Shelter and Welcome

The Story of John Briggs and Mvumi to 1938

Elizabeth McKelvey

JoanRose
Publishing

First published in the United Kingdom in 2008
by JoanRose Publishing

The moral right of the author has been asserted

ISBN 978-0-9560467-0-3

Produced by
Action Publishing Technology Ltd, Gloucester
www.actiontechnology.co.uk

Printed and bound in Great Britain

Contents

Acknowledgements

I am indebted to so many people who have helped me in various ways throughout the research which has led to this book, some of whom I have met, some I have not. Firstly the maps I have used are taken from *Signal on the Mountain: The Gospel in Africa's Uplands before the First World War* (Acorn Press Ltd, 1991). Used by permission of the author, Miss Elisabeth Knox, whom I would like to thank, and whose scholarly book was a huge help in getting me started. In addition Elisabeth kindly sent me copies of the interviews she had made with older people in the Mvumi District in 1968.

I would also like to thank Canon Chidosa and the late Mrs Chidosa with whom I had a number of very helpful conversations. They guided me with their comprehensive knowledge of the people of Mvumi over 80 years and they gave me the confidence that it really was important enough to write down. In addition, Canon Chidosa arranged for me to meet many of the surviving 'wazee' (elders), even accompanying me to people's homes and sitting patiently through each interview.

Many thanks are due to Ken Osborne, the archivist at the Church Mission Society (CMS), and indeed all those before him who have recognised the value of maintaining the records and documents. Ken gave me access to the vast wealth of CMS archives and provided me with some of the images. Staff at the Special Collections of Birmingham University Library, where the CMS archive is kept, were also very helpful.

Dorothy and Hugh Prentice also gave me a helping hand, having me to stay in their home in Kongwa for a week, and giving me access to all of Hugh's historical research papers.

Muriel Meeres, daughter of Ralph Banks, has been very generous in supplying me with copies of her parents photographs and her father's diaries.

Edna Miller, a descendant of Rhoda Briggs's sister, kindly supplied me with copies of the early portraits of the Briggs family.

Members of staff at CMS Australia also helped me in a number of ways, supplying me with some photographs and a copy of the memoirs of Avis Richardson.

Thanks too are due to those who have encouraged me through the long and drawn out process of writing; my husband David, Lizzy, Anne, Lucy, Hannah, to name but a few.

THE USSAGARA MISSION 1913

from a map by Miss Peel

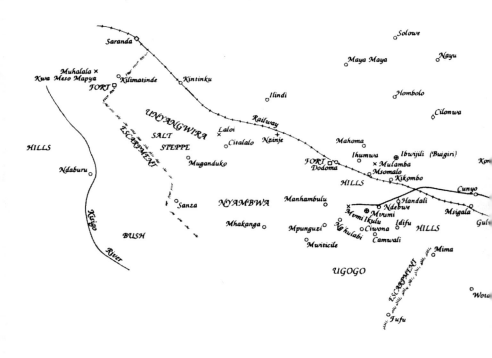

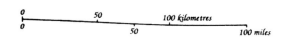

Courtesy of Elisabeth Knox

CHAPTER 1

A Story Worth Telling

There are many questions we would like to ask of those who have gone before us. Why did you leave and never come back? Who was your father? How did you manage? What was she like? We live with the results, and although there may be things we long to go back and change, in other cases it is simply that we would like to know and understand the story. What happened? Why? Maybe the story was never told, words never voiced it, and it was kept within as a very private matter. Or maybe the story was known just as plain fact, and was never thought to be a story worth telling. Perhaps the story was told for a while, but later abandoned as the years passed and the people were forgotten.

So the story went to the grave, the words blown away in the wind, and all we are left with are the physical items, the official records, perhaps letters and photos. Or maybe we have their handiwork; embroidery, lace, sketches, furniture or even buildings. What can these things tell us?

Just as there are marks on the ground left by what has gone before ... this land was farmed in strips ... this pile of cut stones was once a fort ... so the physical things left by those before us can only give us an outline of the story, a hint of the character. This story is the remains of a story, it is like standing amongst excavated ruins, seeing the shape of the rooms, the broken pieces of pot, the fragment of mosaic floor, and imagining the rest. This story is the excavated story of John Henry Briggs, who went to the plains of East Africa and built a home of shelter and welcome on a hill called Mvumi. A young man of no conse-quence went to a place of no riches or importance and spent a lifetime there. Nearly one hundred years later I went to live on that hill. Seeing the quality of his work and hearing the echo of his name, I wanted to uncover what I could. This story is the result of my digging. It is a story that has not been told, but that is exactly why his story is worth telling.

* * *

Ezekiel and Rhoda Briggs were both from Norfolk and worked as domestic servants, he a coachman, she a laundress. They married at St Bride's Church in the City of London on 30th July 1864, presumably working in a grand house there. By the time their first child Elizabeth, known as Lizzie, was born in 1866 they had moved to Great Amwell in Hertfordshire where they remained for a number of years, still as servants. John was born there on the 5th February 1868 and was a pupil at the village school, passing the sixth standard at the age of 13 or 14.

John had always attended Sunday School classes but at about the age of 16 years old the teaching took on personal meaning for him and he became profoundly committed to Christ. He would walk 7 miles every Sunday afternoon to hold an open air meeting in a distant village and then walk home again.

At about the same time as his conversion he was apprenticed to a large firm of wholesale nursery gardeners. He learnt every aspect of the business, later on even travelling for them for a short time over much of England. By the time he was 22 the family unit of four were still together but had moved to an address in Tunbridge Wells – perhaps a move that followed John's employment. John was still with the same company and had earned the title 'nursery gardener', his father was retired and his mother and sister were earning a living with a private laundry business.

John felt the call of missionary service and applied to the Church Missionary Society, an Anglican society, which took up references from many churchmen on his character and qualities, on his suitability for the work. All the references concerning this 22 year old nurseryman were excellent, so the Committee sat and considered his application on 28 October 1890. Probably

Top left
Rhoda & Ezekiel Briggs

Top right
Lizzie Briggs

Left
John Briggs

Courtesy of Edna Miller

because of his relatively low level of education, and perhaps also because of his youth, they decided to ask him to spend several months staying with the Rev Cornford (a CMS representative) helping in the parish, receiving essential Greek tuition and being tested for his missionary potential. The Rev. Cornford too wrote well of him, not only in character but also in ability and in attitude to study: 'Mr John Briggs has now been with me more than 12 weeks . . . that which struck me first is his wholeheartedness to his preparation work'.

At this point, John had one question on his mind before he would make a definite offer and start the next stage of his training, and he wasn't too shy to ask. He wrote to the Committee enquiring about marriage 'not that I am contemplating an early marriage but I want to look forward a little to the future. Would I have to leave if I got married?' Whatever the answer to that question was, he did indeed make a definite offer and he was accepted for further training on the 23 June 1891. Less than a week later he entered the CMS men's training college in Islington where he spent a very busy time.

John was a 'short course' man, normally 1 year and 1 term. Those with more academic inclinations, and with more money to support themselves, could study for longer. The day started early with chapel, then there were 3½ hours of taught lessons: the afternoons were flexible depending on the needs of the student and the evening was for private study and medical lectures.

There was plenty of emphasis on the physical; industrial training saw students learning essential skills in carpentry, blacksmithing, tinsmithing, cobbling, printing and gardening (though perhaps John was excused the latter). Wherever they went, these missionaries would have to build, repair, remake and improvise. The medical lectures were quite extensive covering advanced ambulance training, elementary anatomy, physiology and the treatment of common diseases. For any missionary, regardless of where in the world they were headed, medical training was important not only for the care of themselves and of one another, but also because it was an important way of expressing God's love to the people they would be living amongst. Prevention being better than cure, the missionaries were encouraged to get plenty of exercise, there were teams of fives, football, lawn tennis and, long before such things were fashionable, there was even an in-house gymnasium. A good level of fitness when they left and began the long, and often arduous, journeys that lay ahead could only be a benefit.

John was headed for German East Africa, an area of the CMS work that was becoming fraught with political complications. CMS had sent the first group of men to that area less than twenty years before, in order to establish a route for missionary caravans to get from the east coast of Africa to land-locked Uganda. The route from the coast at Bagamoyo travelling inland to Unyanyembe, (where Stanley had met Livingstone not so long before), had been used by slave caravans and was well recorded so it had been the obvious choice in what was then unknown territory. The mission stations that CMS had planned to establish would be a base for missionary work but would also be a kind of service station, where missionaries bound for Uganda could find rest, and be supplied with food and goods along the way. However in 1890 a new and easier route to Uganda was discovered further north, and once that route was open the handful of missionaries working in German East Africa became peripheral to the focus of work in the region.

At the same time German East Africa had become more firmly under German rule. The few solitary missionaries working there desperately needed help, but since CMS was a British society there was a feeling that to increase the work would anger the Germans and mean that they were thrown out entirely. In addition, without the commitment and support of the governing authority was it a good investment of people and money? It was to this strained and sparse group of missionaries that John was sent.

John's time at Islington was cut short; less than a year after starting, on 9th May 1892 at the grand age of 24 years and 3 months, he joined a party who were leaving for East Africa. He was in the company of David Deekes, a man just a few years older who had already spent 4 years with CMS on the south-eastern side of Lake Victoria. Deekes liked to tell the tale of how he had once entertained Stanley there, serving a tin of cheese

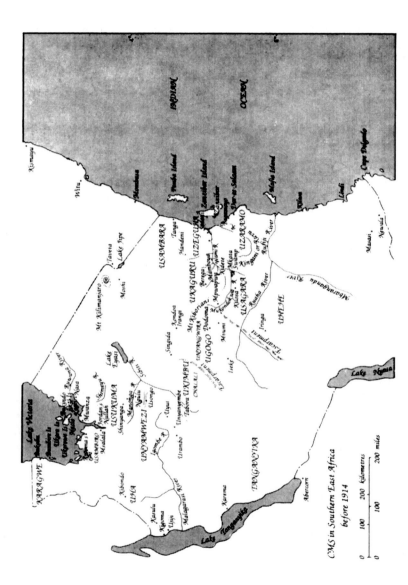

CMS in Southern East Africa
before 1914

0   100   200 Kilometres
0   100   200 miles

Courtesy of Elisabeth Knox

that was so hard it had to be cut with an axe. David was newly married and was starting out with his bride to make a new home in German East Africa. Time spent together on this voyage was the start of a long association.

By June the party had reached Frere Town, a mission station near Mombasa, where John met Rev. and Mrs Wood on their way home for leave after 6 years in German East Africa. They must surely have had some lengthy conversations and John would have picked up a lot of useful information. He also met his Bishop, Bishop Tucker, whose diocese of Eastern Equatorial Africa covered a vast area, so this rare chance to meet must surely have been a valuable one too.

Group of East Africa Missionaries taken at Frre Town in June 1982
Courtesy CMS

A – Bishop Tucker
B – Mrs Wood and baby
C – John Briggs
D – Rev. A N Wood

Some First Impressions of Arriving in East Africa

Life on a Caravan Journey – an account published in the CMS Gleaner Aug 1892

Our difficulties, when we want to move inland begin with the re-packing of our goods. We find that our home boxes are too big, as each man can only carry 60–64 lbs. ... At last the happy moment comes when our provisions, bedstead, blankets, clothing, cooking pots, rice, beads, wire etc are quite ready. The next thing, of course, is to secure porters to carry them and on the fact being made known, we receive applications from men of various tribes, shades and sizes. ... You make an arrangement for the day and hour and they do not show. A two hour delay can mean that you have to spend the night in a place with no water.

With about 100 porters, each having carefully chosen and marked his load, which he keeps to the end of the journey, we start on our way, in Indian file ... Uncomfortable though this slow mode of progression may be, it is undoubtedly picturesque. The long line of dusky figures, on the narrow winding footpath, over an undulating country, the motley costumes, and loads of almost every conceivable shape produce a striking and ever varying effect.

When the camp is settled on, then there is the putting up of tents, collecting firewood, the cook looking for pots and pans, but the provisions haven't arrived yet. By the time to retire, the place is lit by watch fires, and the last stragglers arrive. The headman reports affairs, tells us of one or two that are sick. So loads are readjusted to leave less important things behind, and then we have to provide for the sick man.

Extracts from Ruth Spriggs's diary Jan 1898

From Frere Town we travelled again by boat to Saadani on the mainland coast of German East Africa. At Saadani thanks to the German Custom Officer we were only ten minutes getting from the ship to the shore ... He lent us his boat and it soon got through the surf and the natives carried us ashore. It was quarter of an hours walk to a shelter, a square white washed hut with a corrugated iron roof and cemented floors, which only opened when a safari was going through. We stowed boxes in one room

as they came through customs. It would be used as a tool shed at
home. We had some bread and made some tea. That was
Tuesday. By Friday morning all things were out of the custom
house and the men being appointed to their work we made our
first march to Ndunie.

We rested on Sunday, started again on Monday at 2.30 am.
The tents were struck at 3 am to move at 4 am. At 3 am, as we
Europeans were all ready, Mr Fincher yelled at the top of his
voice 'Hiya! Hiya! Mamboya' and immediately there was an
answering shout and in every direction up sprang the men and
the whole camp was on the move. We did 3 ¼ hour marches
starting at that time for several days but then from Kanu we left
at midnight, it being an 8 hour march to reach water.

The journey up from the coast was several hundred miles, so it
wasn't until 1 October 1892 that John finally arrived at
Mpwapwa and then neighbouring Kisokwe where he was to
make his first home. He wrote back to the Committee reporting
his arrival in a characteristically understated way.

I will not trouble you with an account of my journey up from the
coast. You must have had many accounts of such journeys and
there is a deal of sameness in them; being my first caravan
journey it had the charm of novelty and I enjoyed it immensely
although I was quite alone.

On the journey, unbeknown to John, some of his porters had
stolen property from a village.

I did not find it out until night, when the Chief gathered his
warriors together and came to fight my caravan. I enquired the
cause and then sent for the chief. He came with some of his men
and we formed a circle outside my tent, lighting a fire in the
middle to give us light. He stated his cause for fighting and I sent
my headman to find the thieves. For about three hours I sat there
while the things one by one turned up. Some of the stolen property was sugar cane and chickens which the men had eaten.
There was no way of finding out which were the thieves in this so

I paid for them myself. The Chief and I parted good friends and for a second time that night I went to bed.

It was unusual for a new missionary to travel up-country without the support of fellow missionaries and it was generally to be avoided. John must have travelled with the Deekes's as far as their new home, Mamboya, which was nearer the coast. Only the last hundred miles or so of his journey would have been 'quite alone', but it must have felt a particularly long hundred miles. I wonder if he found the strange and new environment incredibly exciting, and felt the joy of a longing being fulfilled, or whether he doubted himself and his calling and felt utterly overwhelmed.

The caravan route from the coast was a steady climb up the gradual slope of the escarpment that forms much of eastern Africa. Water supply was essential at points along the way, and so at Mpwapwa the route skirted the lower slopes of a range of hills where there was water off the mountains. Arabs had long been passing through on their journeys obtaining slaves, and some of the caravans could have as many as two or three thousand men. Any slaves that managed to escape to the mission compound at Mpwapwa would be given sanctuary and taken in. The local people were friendly to the mission, and even surrounded them with a guard of warriors at such times. Being opposed to the Arabs and undermining their business in this way was a very dangerous thing to do, as they sometimes used force and threats of violence to regain captives and occasionally they succeeded. Being a missionary was certainly not a vocation for cowards.

When John arrived in Mpwapwa he went first to meet his colleague and neighbour, the Rev. J. C. Price. Now in his late thirties, Price had been there for 13 years and had become closely identified with the local people. He was known affectionately by them as Bwana Mwalimu, 'Mr Teacher'. Price had learnt the local language, Chigogo, from simply living alongside the people, and had written a grammar book for those who came to learn the language after him. He had been preaching in their language for 10 years, had written choruses and translated hymns which he set to the native music style, a style which people could easily learn and remember because it was part of their own culture.

The community of people living at Mpwapwa was diverse. Even then the people living in the area included settlers of all kinds, there were porters who had fallen away from caravan journeys, there were slaves living as members of tribal households, and refugees from famine and war. Price ran a school and a number of young people, homeless children and ex-captives of all ages lived in boarding houses under his care. Some had come to him under particularly tragic circumstances. One girl was a slave rescued by the Germans and given to Price to care for, another was picked up in a starving condition by Price on the road 2 miles from Mpwapwa. She had belonged to a caravan going to the coast and been left on the road to die. Another, a youth, had been found as a baby tied to the neck of his dead mother, who had been killed by the Masai. Other children in Price's boarding houses were from more privileged backgrounds: one of the local chiefs, Chief Lukole, had died in 1891, and three of his children were living with Price. One of them, a son called N'honya, was a very promising and able student who was helping Price translate the Bible into Chigogo. Another chief sent his son to live with Price to learn to read, so that he might teach his father.

Since the students were not all of the local tribe, the language used in the school was the more universal trading language of Swahili and the class times had to be short; the local youths had work to do and Price's boarding students also had to farm fields and tend animals. They needed to be self-supporting since the Mission was nearly always short of money.

Price was a remarkable man. Bishop Tucker wrote of him 'It was an object lesson in self-denial to see the way in which Price lived and did his work. It was absolutely true of him that nothing of the things which he possessed did he count his own. He and his flock had all things in common.'* Price shared his food with his household, eating the local foods that they ate, which were not necessarily very nutritious, and even at times adopting local dress. He must have made an enormous impression on John in those first days.

* Quoted in G. A. Chambers, *Tanganyika's New Day*, p.13.

As well as working locally in Mpwapwa, teaching and developing resources in Chigogo, Price had made several expeditions over a number of years deeper into the tribal lands of the Wagogo people on the plains to the west. Leaving in late September 1885, when the terrain was still dry, he had made an eight week trip covering more than 400 miles on foot. He had long conversations with the elders and the people were interested in his message. One chief asked Price to come and live with them 'for his word's sake'. Returning to Mpwapwa, Price passed to the north of some hills from where he glimpsed Mvumi to the south and resolved to return there.

It was another three years, in April 1888, before Price next set out for central Ugogo. He took with him eight porters and goods to trade with. He found receptive people who asked intelligent questions. His porters sang the native style hymns which he had written while he played the concertina. This description gives a flavour of his message.

> One has to try and show them that sin is the real cause of sorrow, and holiness the true ground of joy. Some of them seem to grasp the idea that we can never make our own hearts any better, because we were born with bad hearts, and only God can give us new ones, which is really like being born a second time... Noticing many of the young warriors in my congregation with their broad, glittering spears, I told them that bye and bye they would be making them into hoes ... when war is dead. God has made his son the greatest Chief of all the world, and he wants all men ... to obey him now.

In many places he visited, he found a readiness to listen, and even to accept Christ as their Chief. He returned to Mpwapwa, exhausted by the long march, but later that year he paid two more visits to the Ugogo plains. Sometimes encouraged, sometimes despairing, he prayed 'for the power of the Holy Spirit among these Wagogo.' By the end of the year there was dreadful famine, and some places were nearly deserted as many had fled, looking for food. He wrote of a man who challenged him: 'I suppose it is you who have been to Msomalo and told the people there about this Gospel, and they profess to believe it, but what are they the better for it? They have hunger and get sick and die just like anybody else.'

There was considerable political unrest in the area in the time following that visit, as the African people did not take kindly to the often brutal German rule and rebellion was in the air. Price was unable to visit the area again for three years lest he be mistaken for a German, but in late 1891, not long before John Briggs arrived, Price made another safari and went as far as Mvumi Ikulu, the seat of the chief of Mvumi. He went with six of his young men to help with the preaching, and with two donkeys to help with the loads. These two donkeys had been a gift to Price from a trader; he didn't have the money to buy such luxuries. Most of the people remembered him and made Price very aware of the opportunity that lay open if only he had more support and could spend half the year in Ugogo. Price returned to Mpwapwa, to his translation work and school.

After John's arrival Price wrote a letter back to CMS in London.

> On 3rd October I took him to Kisokwe and introduced him to the people and the work there. From what I have seen of him I think we shall get along capitally together (only together means 6 miles apart!) ... The Wahehe have been fighting in Usagara again this year. They killed the German officer and destroyed lots of villages. Now they talk of coming to Mpwapwa. I have just put a grass roof on in time for them to burn the house if they come! They can't, however, do anything more than our God allows them to. I am not in the least anxious.

Price's attitude to such problems, one of complete trust in the heavenly King, can only have been an inspiration to such a young missionary in his first impressionable months. Price was the only one to whom John could turn with all the questions of a newcomer and he must have had a huge influence on John's thinking at that early stage. John describes the same event:

> I had a hearty welcome from the people here [Kisokwe]. They came halfway to Mpwapwa to meet me. The mission buildings were in a wretched condition, they have all but fallen down. One

could see through the roof and the white ants made their 'hills' inside. When the rains commenced I had to put all my things in a heap on the floor and overthrow with the groundsheet of a tent, my bed into a waterproof bag. One night my stores got buried by a piece of the wall which fell. There were other things in the house besides white ants. I killed two snakes, one a large black cobra five feet long and nearly as thick as ones wrist. I commenced building a new house soon after getting here ... this is nearly finished now ... I have not yet been able to do any teaching as the language is still a difficulty, but have been able to attend to the wants of the body. Ulcers abound and I have vaccinated seven or eight hundred. Small pox is very bad, in some villages nearly all the people have died. Often some dozen or two people will come to be vaccinated and say that all the rest of the people in their village are 'finished' (dead with small pox).

What strength of character and faith it will have taken to deal with the incredible demands of that situation; lonely, grim and desperate, but instead of going running back to Mpwapwa John set to work, functioning and taking constructive action.

John's immediate predecessor at Kisokwe had been Mr Pratley, a missionary with a number of years experience in Frere Town. He

Sketch of mission house, Kisokwe by Bishop Tucker. *Courtesy CMS*

had travelled out with a new recruit, Redman, who had died at Saadani just after landing. Mr Pratley continued to Kisokwe arriving in good health on 4 March, but two days later was seized with fever and died on the 16 March. The shadow of these events only a few months earlier must have affected how John felt, alone, in his new home. He wrote 'on December 24ᵗʰ Mr and Mrs Cole arrived here and my solitary missionary life ended. I was very pleased as it was hard being here and not able to teach the people and no one else to do it.' Henry Cole was an old hand, having first arrived in Mpwapwa with Price many years before, and had just returned from home leave. He was an Irish agriculturalist, so not only was he experienced and knowledgeable but he and John shared an interest in the mission garden.

Though John had only spent three months living on his own, it was three long months when every experience was new and even the chores of daily living were not yet routine. It was a very hard initiation. Had he ever lived on his own before? Communicating was difficult for him and understanding the people's thinking was impossible for him, so such a lonely posting was a considerable test. Of course there were plenty of local people and they were his teachers and carers. John was continually dependent upon them for their good will and protection, like a baby thrust into the world and dependent on its mother.

John continued to put his practical building skills to use; being thrown in the deep end and de-skilled as he was, it must have been wonderful for him to be able to do something useful. Cole wrote from Kisokwe in Nov 1893 that 'under the superintendence of Mr Briggs a substantial stone church has been built, capable of holding four or five hundred people.' (The remains of this church, built simply and graciously of earth and stone, still stands to this day.)

In early 1894 Rev. Beverley returned from home leave with his new bride. John reported:

For some three months my time has been all taken up with building. It was necessary to build a house for Mr Beverley, and as we had no men capable of laying a stone straight who would work, we had to do it ourselves. This was no great hardship. Variety is always pleasant. Our chief regret was the waste of time.

John, an immensely capable practical man, so enjoyed the change from struggling with learning the language and from teaching the local people with only slow progress. John was the underdog in this group of missionaries, all of whom were more formally educated than he was. It was important to him to see these practical jobs done well; working together with Beverley made it satisfying and sociable work as well as a chance, perhaps, to prove his worth.

There were the two languages to learn. Firstly Swahili, the language of caravaning and of wider travel, and secondly the tribal language, Chigogo. There were many demands (including building) made on his time, and books were few so even after John had been in residence for a long 18 months it was still reported that 'Briggs is quite delighted that Beverley is helping him with the language. Now he says he should know something of it.'

During 1894 John, together with Beverley, went to hold open-air services in some of the villages nearby, trying to take along one or two of the native Christians with them to share in the teaching and witnessing. John started a new little school in Idero, a nearby village, where he undertook simple teaching. He did another practical job at Kisokwe, the doctoring, saying in his Annual Letter about it 'and a very busy and interesting time I had in that particular department. If the people are careless and indifferent about receiving our message of Salvation, they are quite ready for the medicine, and come to us to be doctored for every little ache.'

Hardships seemed to be compounding. The people were entirely dependent on their own crops and herds for food. The rainy season in that region lasts only a few months, roughly from December to March, and then there is not a drop of rain for eight or even nine months. In 1891 rinderpest had reduced the size of the herds, in 1893 smallpox swept through, followed by failed rains. John, the gardener, felt powerless to help either the people in their need of food, or the tiny Church in its struggle to stand in the face of such a difficult situation. He wrote in his 1894 Annual Letter:

> Everybody is in a state of semi-starvation, and some rather beyond that. Will you please remember us in prayer at this time, that our Christians may be kept faithful under this great trial and that God may open out some means of sustaining the people. Also that God may pour out His Spirit upon our Native Christians and make them on fire for the conversion of their fellow-countrymen. ... And pray for us workers, that we may know more of His power in our lives and work.

At the same time Price wrote his last Annual Letter, starting on a note of thankfulness 'for enabling me to hold on here another year, and for giving me improved health. I am thankful too that I am no longer alone, ... to have had the companionship of a man like Mr Doulton for the last six months has been a real help and blessing.' Doulton was a well-connected Englishman, who had left his home for Australia as a rebel and then been converted. He was a well-built mature man and an excellent evangelist. It is good to know Price had the blessing of good company because the situation was more than difficult. He continued his letter in a less happy tone:

> The famine ... is the worst I have known during the fifteen years I have been in Africa. It is most distressing, especially as one has little or nothing to help them with. In consequence, a good deal of our work is practically at a standstill. We have had to give up Sunday-school, and only get the few children living about the Mission at the day-school. Our attendances on Sundays are very poor, and outdoor preaching has been given up. The people are all scattered, searching in the forest for wild fruits and roots. The rains have set in well, so that in two or three months the famine ought to be practically over, but the locusts are swarming again, and in some places have already eaten off the young corn. Our God has doubtless some wise and loving purpose in it all, but it is hard for the people to believe that He loves them, under such circumstances, and one feels *so* helpless.

Price had been suffering recurrent bouts of illness for a number of years. He had previously refused to go on home leave and recover his strength, saying to Bishop Tucker 'how is it possible to leave my people when this terrible famine is upon them?' Price had pushed his endurance to the limit, and this latest severe famine eroded his health still further. John had nursed him at times until Doulton arrived. Price died on 23 January 1895 of a liver infection compounded by his poor diet. Doulton wrote back to CMS about these events.

> Our dear brother was only ill four days. On Sunday he appeared very unwell but as this was not unusual with him I did not anticipate anything serious. At night he had a good deal of fever then a terrible shivering fit, the following afternoon he seemed much worse and had another shivering fit. On Tuesday morning Briggs came over and we also had a visit from the German doctor who declared Mr Price to be dangerously ill. He was very bad all that day and night and on Wednesday morning Beverley arrived. Acting under the advice of the German doctor who appeared to understand the case we did all that was possible but all our efforts were unavailing. Our brother was quite unconscious all that day and on Wednesday night at 10.00 he received his home call and entered into rest. We buried him in his own garden. The Native Christians round the grave sang 'safe in the arms of Jesus' and some of them appeared to be deeply affected. It may only be said that his was an unselfish life, he lived for others ... during the short time that I knew him many are the little acts of kindness of which I have been the recipient. If ever a man laid down his life for others, dear Mr Price truly did for the Wagogo.

The grave of J. C. Price, situated as it was then in his garden, is now in the grounds of Mpwapwa Cathedral. The inscription on his grave is not in English but in Chigogo, and translated reads as follows:

In memory of Bwana Teacher
(John Charles Price)
who preached to the Gogo people of Mpwapwa the words of God for fifteen years.
His call by God to rest with Him came on January 23 1895.
Be faithful unto death, and I will give you the crown of life. Revelation 2:10.

The death of Price was a severe blow to the little group of missionaries, and no less a blow to those who he had taken in under his care. John stayed with Doulton to keep him from being lonely – though interestingly no one had ever seemed to worry about John being lonely in his early days. Doubtless there was a lot of work involved in keeping Price's household and school going and that would be too much for the new arrival. By August John had moved permanently to Mpwapwa and the two men worked very well together, the start of another long association.

To continue the story of Mr Doulton and Mr Briggs we need to go back a little in time and learn something of two other new recruits. When Mr and Mrs Beverley arrived in February 1894, they had travelled from England in a party with the returning Mr and Mrs Wood, and two single women, Rose Colsey aged 26 and Ellen Waite aged 34. These were the first single women to be sent by CMS to this part of Africa, a sign of confidence that the region was considered safe enough for single ladies. The two women were placed together at Mamboya, (100 miles away from Mpwapwa, you remember) with the Woods and the Deekes.

Ellen was appointed to take charge of the dispensary at Mamboya and, though diffident about her ability, she applied herself to furthering her knowledge through studying books sent out to her by friends. At times her nursing skills were needed by those at Kisokwe, and when she was called for the two bachelors would go to escort her over the five or six day journey. When the crisis was over the two men would escort her back to her home. (Of course it would be improper for one bachelor to escort her.)

Rose, the younger of the two, was from Tewkesbury in Gloucestershire. Her mother died when she was still very young and her father, an Innkeeper, died just weeks before her fourteenth birthday leaving her in the care of her two older brothers. The eldest was Thomas, a newspaper reporter, who became the head of the house at just eighteen years of age. Her second brother, John, was fifteen years old and was a draper's apprentice. What course Rose's life took over the next few years we don't know, and the records of how she came to offer herself for missionary service are lost. Perhaps the fact that her parents had both died meant that she was free from domestic responsibilities and able to respond to the great needs in Africa that she heard about.

Rose and Ellen had help in language learning from the able Mr Wood, they also had each other to practise with so they were able to make good progress. Quite soon after arriving Rose wrote that she had spent the mornings in language study and the afternoons teaching different classes of scholars. 'The course of instruction is at present very simple: reading, singing, and teaching hymns and portions of Scripture, always closing with a simple Gospel address.' A year later Rose described regularly visiting people in their homes:

> Generally I try and get one gathering in each village, and sometimes the children sing a hymn with me, or repeat a verse of Scripture, and this forms the basis for a talk with the older women. At other times they are busy, and I go from house to house, talking to two or three at a time: then there are often sick ones to be attended to, and the morning has gone all too soon.

By 1897 she was well established, and in her Annual Letter she reported:

> The past year ... has been a very happy one, quite the happiest I have spent out here, although I have had more fever than in former years. ... During the year we have passed ten pupils up to the New Testament reading class, and as, of course, our chief aim is to teach them to read God's Word for themselves, we rejoice at every one who makes progress, yet the fact that so few have been passed on out of an average attendance of seventy-six, will give you some idea of the extreme denseness of the majority of the scholars. Day after day they learn the same syllable; we do indeed need great patience in this work of teaching. ... I have been able to visit regularly among the people, and feel that this is a very real help in keeping up the class and school, and I am most thankful for being thus able to know something of those we reach in their own homes.

Ernest Doulton won Ellen's hand and once permission had been given from the CMS committee and the Bishop they could make plans to go to Zanzibar to be married. Zanzibar had a British consulate where their marriage could be recognised in British law, but in order to marry there they first had to be resident in Zanzibar for three weeks. Put that together with the four week journey down to the coast and the four weeks back, and getting married became a three month trek. Their courtship had obviously been good preparation! John Briggs and Ernest Doulton left Mpwapwa on 28th July 1897, John for his first trip back to England after five years away and Doulton to be married. Mr and Mrs Doulton arrived back in Mamboya in October to keep the work there going, but in March 1898 they returned to Mpwapwa. Rose missed their friendship and counsel very much but she had a new companion in Ruth Spriggs, a short lively woman known by all the local people as 'Bibi Nusu', which best translates as 'lady half'.

Impressions of life in Mamboya

Extracts from Ruth Spriggs's diary:

Rats continue to thrive ... we caught about six last week.

I was sick but got better before the Doctor arrived (sent for on Tuesday, arrived Friday evening). By brandy, port wine and eggs, Brands essence and quinine with God's blessing, Miss Colsey had pulled me through.

We hang meat on the baraza [verandah] under thick thatch, there's plenty of breeze and it keeps from Monday to Saturday.

You see, in this country you take all your furniture with you, as your friends are not, as a rule, able to provide you with any.

John's leave was slightly longer than the usual one year, since while he was in England his father died. He wrote to the Committee asking to extend his stay: 'my mother feels the shock very much and I know she also feels very keenly my going away so soon ... I trust you will see that this is an exceptional circumstance particularly as I am an only son.' He arrived back at Mpwapwa in December of 1898.

Rose remained at Mamboya for her first five years, teaching

the various classes and visiting people in their homes. She must have enjoyed keeping animals, since she had a pet monkey there who was very tame, and she also kept three parrots. She had taken in outcast children and a number of escaped slaves whose freedom she then secured. One of these in particular was a great source of help and encouragement, of whom she wrote:

> You have already heard that in March we had the joy of witnessing the first baptism here in the Valley. Stamile, .. is now as Persisi, beloved by everybody, and is always delighted to labour for her Lord and Saviour. She is a true voluntary helper. Somehow the people go to her quite naturally, and tell her their troubles, difficulties, and desires, and it is just as natural for me to tell her all about the work and seek her help and advice.

Rose writes warmly in her letters of many of the local people she had got to know, and though she is honest about the tests to her patience she writes with fondness and regard. Rose left for home leave in early 1899, very soon after John returned.

On the 29 June 1899 a new diocese was created, when Bishop Peel was consecrated Bishop of Mombasa in St Paul's Cathedral. Rose was very possibly present at that great event, but it certainly had a big effect on those working in the region. Now they had a Bishop with a much smaller area to cover, who only had hundreds of miles to travel from his base in Mombasa in order to visit them; a real advocate for them, with experience himself of being a missionary in India. Shortly after, a group of missionaries meeting in Mamboya wrote to the 'Parent Committee' in London suggesting that at least two men should live and work in the plains of Ugogo, west of Mpwapwa. This was an area which had only received occasional visits but which, it was felt, was a promising area for work. They asked for money to build a temporary building in a well populated centre. This request was granted, but they were told that the cost of building should not exceed £100.

CHAPTER 2

Haya Haya Mvumi
1900–1904

The year of 1900 was a big year for John Henry Briggs; not only was he given the job of pioneering a new station, but it was also the year he married. Now with considerable experience and language skills behind him, in practical matters always capable, and blessed with a strong constitution, he stood on the threshold of exciting new things. As Bishop Peel later related: 'A march of just under fifty miles will take one from Mpwapwa to Mvumi, but I imagine Mr Briggs is the only one who has covered the ground in sixteen hours.' Imagine that! John was becoming a valuable and respected member of the missionary band.

The previous year John had been on an itinerating journey west into Ugogo, the tribal land of the Gogo people, and in February he returned there.

> I went to Mvumi .. and was favourably received by the chief and people. My object was to make them understand what our purpose in building a house meant, and they expressed them-selves as ready to receive us as teachers, come to be taught, and send their children to school. My visit extended over a week, and when I left I arranged to supply teachers from Mpwapwa who would go for a month at a time for visiting and school work.

Rose returned from her home leave in March 1900 and travelled in the company of Bishop Peel as he made a first visit to his new diocese. In the 10 weeks that he spent in the region he walked an incredible 800 miles. Bishop Peel was quite a small man, very energetic and able, he preferred to walk himself rather than to be carried in a hammock as some were, and was able to cover the ground fast. He was committed to the people and the work.

Left to right, back row: Rose Colsey, Rev. Rees, John Briggs, Rev. Fincher, David Deekes, Rev. Wood.
Front row: Mrs Rees, Bishop Peel, Mrs Wood, Ruth Spriggs.
Courtesy CMS

On 5 and 6 April 1900 all 10 missionaries currently on the field met together with Bishop Peel at Mamboya. This included John, Rev Fincher from Kisokwe, Miss Spriggs, Rose, Rev. and Mrs Rees, Mr and Mrs Deekes and Rev. and Mrs Wood, all of Mamboya. It was an exciting few days, and apart from the decisions being made in the meetings something else was going on behind the scenes; John and Rose became engaged. The picture above was taken in the few days that this group were together, at the time that their engagement was announced, and you can nearly see the excitement in John's pose. The Rev. David Rees is standing between them, the man who was later to marry them – perhaps this too had just been arranged.

As you may remember getting married was not such a

straightforward procedure. Since John had been back on the field for a year or so he needed to get a medical certificate from a suitably qualified doctor, and the German doctor was away. Rose had just returned from leave so she had recently satisfied the medical authorities as to her soundness of mind and body. In addition, even though the Bishop gave his blessing, John needed to request permission to marry Rose from the Parent Committee in London, and he wrote to them on 20 April. The letter arrived in London on 11 June, and it wasn't until mid-August that he and Rose received the reply.

Meanwhile the Bishop's visit continued at a pace. His report gives a vivid account:

From April 25th to May 4th Mr Briggs and I were on the march in Ugogo. We reached Mvumi. The proposed site for the new mission-house was to be inspected there on April 27th. We camped on a knoll about a mile distant from the Chief's tembe. Chief Masenha soon visited us. He offered a large piece of the knoll to the Society if we would build there and teach the tribe. We could see no better site for miles around, and with some misgivings agreed to put up a trial house. We desired still higher ground. Hills banked up the horizon on all sides. Millet fields decked the plain, the stalks of the grain being from 10ft to 15ft high. The tembes were quite hidden by the little forest of corn-blades. A dry river-bed tortuously broke the surface of the open piece of plain at the foot of our knoll. Fresh water, good (?) and salt water abounded. Within three-quarters of a mile were some open stretches yielding salt. Trees and bushes, save some thorny ones, were very scarce. Stone lay to hand. Two or three miles away was limestone ... All things carefully considered we turned the first sod of the excavations for the foundations of the new mission house at this post, fifty miles beyond Kisokwe. The great number of people under Masenha, so friendly to us, induced us to thus settle down. Twenty thousand people must be within easy reach and are willing to listen to us.

It is not mentioned by Bishop Peel or John Briggs at the time, but it is remembered locally, that the hill Masenha gave to them had been the site of a battle between the Wagogo and the fierce Wahehe whose land was further south. The hill was covered in bones and as a result nobody wanted to live there. The hill happened to be visible from the chief's house a few miles away, so perhaps the local chief felt he would be able to keep an eye on the goings on there without being disturbed too much himself. John gave his report of the events that followed:

> The Bishop's visit to Ugogo was a great cause for thankfulness; from the time when the late Rev. J. C. Price used to pay yearly visits there it has been felt that more should be done for the Wagogo than these isolated itinerations. ... While at Mvumi the Bishop saw the site proposed for a house there, and approved it. Foundations were at once marked out on a plan drawn up by him, and work begun.
>
> Kisokwe claimed a share of my time while the building of the house at Mvumi, which I had been asked to undertake, and to which new station I was appointed by Bishop and Committee, had also to be done and which the distance of fifty miles from Mpwapwa made a somewhat arduous task. Two journeys were made there for that purpose, with a stay of a month or so each time ... The building left little time for direct spiritual effort or school work, and nothing beyond Sunday services and visiting of villagers on Sundays could be done. However I got round to a good many places, and the number of workpeople employed kept one in touch with the people. Building wood is unobtainable in Mvumi, and getting it from other districts was an opportunity of taking to them the Gospel. I spent a week at Camwato for that purpose, a place which has never been visited or preached in before, and had the joy of declaring to people who had never heard it the good news of a full and free salvation.
>
> While at Mvumi the openings for medical work were brought vividly before one. I had no medicines to speak of and so most of the people had to be told that I could not treat them. One case was especially sad. A little Masai boy was brought who had been badly bitten by a hyaena. I washed his wounds and did an extensive amount of sewing up, and then I wanted dressings, but these I hadn't got. I had to send him home to be looked after as best they could by his parents.

In June the German doctor returned and was satisfied that John was likely to stand the climate and was fit to be married. The

Bishop had hoped that they might be able to have a civil
wedding with a German registrar but this was not possible, so
they too had to make the trek to Zanzibar to be married before
the British Consul. They left Mamboya for the coast on 20
September 1900, Rose accompanied by Persisi, the baptised
Mamboya woman mentioned earlier, and Mr Deekes went as
escort. Rose and John were finally married at the Zanzibar
(British) Consulate on 27 October 1900, and then set off on their
return journey to walk up-country, arriving back at Mamboya a
whole two months after leaving.

Rose and John
Courtesy of Edna Miller

Mamboya was Rose's home and so it was in the church there
that they married in the religious ceremony that they considered
to be more important. Rees married them, Deekes gave Rose
away and the newly returned Henry Cole was the best man.
Remarkably neither Rose nor John refer to their marriage in
their annual letters for the year, but thankfully Henry, the Irish-
man, thought it was an occasion worth reporting.

The first English wedding in Usagara took place on the 23rd of last month (Nov) when Mr Briggs and Miss Colsey were joined together in the bonds of holy matrimony. The Natives were greatly exercised in their minds as to the amount of dowry paid by the bridegroom, and when told that the alliance was simply a matter of mutual love, without any commercial signification, they were both surprised and amused.

Extracts from Ruth Spriggs's diary

The wedding of Miss Colsey to Mr Briggs went off very well. . . . The natives were as quiet as mice, and so orderly. Mr Cole left the same evening . . . and then Mr and Mrs Briggs started for Mvumi, their station, by going for a short march first.

The new Mr and Mrs Briggs headed straight for Mvumi, stopping over a few days to change porters at Mpwapwa and doubtless to pick up John's possessions and finish up any last matters there. The new couple arrived in Mvumi on 6 December 1900 to take up residence, although the house was not quite completely finished. Within two weeks Rose was seriously ill with blackwater fever (severe malaria), made a recovery and then relapsed. It was only in mid-January that she was reported to be convalescing. She had been travelling for two and a half months, often in very feverish places, and this took its toll on her previously excellent health.

John and Rose may have been a cornerstone of the new station but they took along with them quite a number of people. Earlier in the year John had promised to send visiting teachers to Mvumi, who would go for a month at a time, so probably during the year, whilst John was building and still supervising the work at Mpwapwa, there had been teaching and preaching underway by teachers from Mpwapwa. It is possible that on the great occasion of the move from Mpwapwa John and Rose formed a caravan and a number of others travelled with them. Perhaps they had a service of prayer and dedication before they left. 'Haya, haya, Mvumi'! What an exciting journey. Who may have been in that caravan arriving on 6 December that symbolised the birth of Mvumi Mission?

Mvumi Mission House
Courtesy of CMS

Benyamini and Dorika Mulugu came at the beginning with their son Mika. Benyamini is remembered as a small dark man who was born at Chimagayi. Dorika was of the Sagala tribe from Kilosa who had come to live at Chimagayi for some reason. They lived in Mvumi until 1911 when they were requested to go to Mvumi Makulu to live as teachers. They remained there until old age. Benyamini was a very gentle, welcoming and jolly man; in his conversation he liked just to talk about God. He especially liked to teach the children songs and little games, and they in turn liked him.

Pawulo and Rebekah Cidinda were also amongst the first to come. It is remembered that Pawulo was a Ugandan by tribe, and to look at he was very dark skinned and tall. It is believed that he came with his two younger brothers, Mtandale Makali and Javan Makali who later settled near Mima – perhaps they escaped from a slave caravan or perhaps they tried working as porters and then settled down.

Lazaro Hembokamu has been consistently named as someone who came at the beginning with John from Mpwapwa but not more is known about him than this. It is said that his mental powers deteriorated years later, perhaps with an illness, and so he ceased to teach.

Rose's trusted companion Persisi, who had accompanied her to Mombasa, together with her husband Ibrahimu Ferusi came from Mamboya and stayed for the first year.

Andereya and Hagulwa Lungwa came with their children, Sala (born c.1891), Ester (born 1895) and Petro, who was born only the previous year and was a baby carried to Mvumi on his mothers back. Hagulwa was a cousin of Benyamini Mulugu, and Andereya was one of the teachers, and an able man. John wrote about him: 'Andreya Lungwa came under the influence of the Rev. J. C. Price at Mpwapwa, and after working for some years as a servant was trained by him as a teacher.' He caused great disappointment within a few weeks after arriving when John had to report that Andereya had fallen into sin (adultery). Andereya worked as a laundryman for a few years before proving himself again. Andereya and Hagulwa went on to have several more children, one of whom, Rosa, was baptised in 1909 and was still alive and living in Mvumi in 1999.

There is also a story about Tadayo Mwano, who came with his wife Rabeka and their children, Salama (born c. 1894), and Talitha (born c. 1897). Tadayo was himself of the Nyaturu tribe from further inland. One day, as a small boy, Tadayo had been out herding the goats when all of a sudden an Arab slave caravan appeared. He was caught by the Arabs and included among their slaves. This slave caravan travelled around a lot and Tadayo was made to be their personal servant. In their travels many of the other slaves were sold off until there were only two left, Tadayo and a young girl. The caravan reached Mpwapwa where they stayed for a few weeks, but towards the end of that time Tadayo heard that they would be leaving in three days and going to the coast. This news made him decide to run away to the mountains where he stayed for those three days just eating wild fruits. Finally he came back down the mountain and went to Chief Chipanjilo's house where he explained his story and that he hadn't been bought by the Arabs, but taken. The Chief received him and gave him protection and from then on Tadayo considered himself a member of that tribe.

Tadayo was looked after well by a man called Cibaya and his wife Rabeka. When smallpox came Cibaya became sick with it, and Tadayo nursed him in a camp in isolation from the rest of the people. Sadly Cibaya did not recover and when Rabeka's younger sister became infected, Tadayo nursed her too. She recovered but Tadayo became sick. He also recovered although quite badly marked, and permanently losing the use of his right eye. He then married Rabeka, since he had become like a brother to Cibaya. They were closely associated with the missionaries at Mpwapwa, being of Chipanjilo's family, and Tadayo was baptised there by Rev. Cole in 1900. He joined John, his teacher, as a porter and settled down in Mvumi farming and turning his hand to whatever was required.

Secelela Nhizwa was amongst that early group. She had been baptised by Price a number of years before and was married to Nataneli Nhonya, Chief Chipanjilo's son, who had been Price's favourite pupil. They already had a daughter Mwendwa (born c.1895) and young son Stefano Tomi. Their family group also included a youth called Hezekiah Luhusa who had come to Mpwapwa from Hombolo with other family members looking for food (possibly in the severe famine of 1894). The others all died and Hezekiah was left alone. Nataneli was out hunting, found the boy and took him in as his own. Their daughter Akisa, was still alive in Mvumi in 1999.

Simeyoni and Raheli Camulomo came too; Simeyoni was John's herdsman in Mpwapwa and was able to read enough to teach the 'cloth class', that is, teaching the syllables which were sewn onto a large cloth. John had many cattle and took delivery of a bucket of milk every morning. Simeyoni continued to look after the animals in Mvumi.

Mika and Abigeli Muloli came; Abigeli was Secelela's younger sister. Secelela and Abigeli had come with their parents from a place called Uzaganza between Mpwapwa and Kilosa. The family had gone to Mpwapwa to work for the missionaries. Mika was from Nghulabi, and had been called to the Mpwapwa district by his relative Simeyoni Camulomo. Mika was already a teacher at Mpwapwa and later recalled that he was then paid six rupees a month for that work. He and Abigeli are thought to have made the move to Mvumi in 1905, but Mika may well have helped by visiting and teaching before then.

Edward Tumbo came as a cook with his wife Abijaili; Abijaili was the younger sister of Rabekah Mwano, mentioned above, who had been nursed by Tadayo and recovered. Some others known to have come from Mpwapwa include Ananiya Ibrahimu (a builder) and his wife Zipporah, and Enoci and Ada Musambili.

Many of these people had been baptised already at Mpwapwa or at Kisokwe, while others were not yet baptised when they came to Mvumi, but were baptised over the following years. For example Edward and Abijaili Tumbo were baptised in Mvumi in August 1904, and Ananiya and Zipporah Ibrahimu were baptised in Mvumi in March 1908.

There were others too, some young single people, but these are all the names remembered. They came as apprentice teachers and evangelists; as porters and builders; as farmers and livestock keepers and houseworkers. For John and Rose, they were people who they knew and could depend on, people who knew their work and would be loyal to them, people who were at least to some extent, for the gospel. For John and Rose they were friends. It is recalled that John provided them with tembes (traditional mud roof houses), married people had their own houses, the young women and the young men had some houses too, but far away from each other within the mission centre. The group of people who came must have had considerable trust in John and Rose, to be prepared to leave what they knew and the place where they were known and go somewhere else. John looked after them, helped them pay taxes, and paid them for work done. They were a group of surprisingly mixed tribal origins, and in this uprooting and replanting a new identity was being formed. Those who were under John's chieftainship became known as 'watu wa Briggs', Briggs's people. There was already quite a bit of inter-relationship between them, and in the next generation that was to become even more so as their children inter-married, staying within the new tribal group. Even today their descendants are referred to as 'watu wa Briggs'.

The received memory of these descendants is that there was a fight amongst some of the Christian community at Mpwapwa, and one woman was killed. There were two incidents, the first involving an Mnyatura woman called Nzungha, who was cared for by the missionaries. She had a short leg though she was able to walk on it and had gone out to the toilet at night (this would be the field), where she was killed by a youth called Tulo who said she was a witch. The second incident was the murder of a Christian man who was shot through a window while eating his supper by himself, he had no wife. Again it was said that he was a witch. It was remembered that the missionaries were angry about people in the mission community being killed – and since the Christian group was still very small perhaps this was a contributory factor in bringing quite a large group of people to a new start in Mvumi.

Once Rose recovered her health she had to start learning a new language, Cigogo. Mamboya was in a different tribal area so all her Kaguru language would be of little use now. She had already learnt two languages, now she needed to learn a third.

It wasn't long before John and Rose started receiving visitors. Ruth Spriggs recorded in her diary on 30 May 1901 that following a conference at Mpwapwa she went with Mr and Mrs Deekes to Mvumi for a holiday. 'It was a real rest and change to be there. Mr Briggs had a rather bad attack of malarial fever while we were there but otherwise it was a most enjoyable holiday.'

As 1901 progressed the Mission work became more established. John reported at the end of the year that since the previous year had been so much occupied with building it was this year that should be looked upon as the beginning of a new work. He sent a detailed description of how they had spent the year:

Visiting. – After a while we were able to arrange twice a week whole day visits to some of the further places. Our plan was to start early in the morning on our donkeys and go to some place about two hours away. We visited and, if possible, had a meeting. At noon we rested where we could for lunch … after an hour or two of such rest and refreshment, I try and get a big meeting, and then mount our donkeys and ride home.

Services. – Through lack of workers (native) we have only been able to have Sunday services at one centre. At first they were held on our verandah, then later in a temporary church. We have just built a more permanent place which will seat 300. We have service twice on Sundays; a shortened form of Morning and Evening Prayer is read, and plenty of singing. This is followed by an address on one of the parables or miracles. That of the afternoon is largely devoted to catechizing on what was taught in the morning. Sometimes we have as many as 120 present, but our average is about eighty.

Classes. – We have two classes in the week, one for Christians and catechumens, and one for inquirers. Our Christians and catechumens are all from Mpwapwa, and are our servants. We have nine inquirers, the result of our work here. They are all men and three of them are past middle age. They listen attentively when being taught, and considering how material their ideas are, and have been from their youth up, they really assimilate a good deal of it. We hope and pray that these first-fruits from Mvumi may be taught of the Holy Spirit, and that they may be brought out and called by Him to be witnesses and the future home missionaries in Mvumi.

Schools. – We have school three times a week for two hours in the afternoon. This is managed by my wife. The attendance varies very much; sometimes as many as seventy come, but the average is thirty-five. The plan followed is: a New Testament reading class first for all who can read. While this is going on the people are gathering, and then school is opened with a hymn and prayer. The majority of the scholars are still at the cloth (a sheet on which is printed the syllables). Some few have got into the first reading book. This goes on for an hour and then a Scripture lesson is given or a hymn taught, and school closes with singing and prayer. We have been unable to open more schools, as we have had no teachers to send to them. ... After meetings held in Mpwapwa last June, two young men volunteered for work here and were engaged as probationary agents by the Executive Committee. They came to us at the end of August. We believe them to be really earnest fellows, but they have a very poor knowledge of the Bible and are generally very ignorant. We have felt it necessary to let them spend a good deal of their time in study, and so to lay a good foundation for future work. They help in school and go out visiting three times a week with the principal object of collecting the children.

Medical. – At the beginning of the year we had no medicine at Mvumi. However, last May Dr Baxter kindly sent us a load from Mamboya, and since that time we have had dispensary days three times a week. The attendance averages about fifty weekly. Ulcers are especially numerous. We commence dispensary hour with an address, generally given by one of our native helpers, and after that the patients are treated.

Itinerating. – Mvumi is such an immense field – to say nothing of the other places around – that much of it can only be reached by living in a tent. We spent altogether five weeks this year in camp. Our plan is to select as good a centre as possible and pitch our tent under a tree, if there is one near. Our safari generally attracts attention and the people come to see who we are. We get the tent up quickly .. when we have got straight we get the organ out and my wife begins to play. This generally brings a crowd, and, if it is a new place to us, their attempts at singing and their evident enjoyment of it must be seen and heard to be appreciated. The nearest villages are next visited and the people invited to collect together for a service. Meanwhile small parties keep coming in; each must have the organ played for them. When they gather, some time is spent teaching them the words of a hymn, then to sing it. A simple address, or perhaps explanation of the hymn learnt follows, and then, when we see they have kept quiet as long as they can, we sing again. Afterwards questions are asked and discussion invited, and the answers given and the questions asked often show that they have followed closely what has been said.

These itinerations, or camping safaris around the district, were features of John's life throughout his years in Mvumi. The Briggs entourage on such a trip would comprise something like three servants to assist with the work of living (collecting water, cooking), a donkey or two, then twelve porters with loads and a boy to look after the donkeys. Following at the back was the 'mnyapara' who had to look after the porters and arrange their loads. There was camp equipment to carry, (tents, camp beds and chairs, pots and pans) as well as food, teaching materials, and also medical supplies with which to treat people. Rose was carried in a chair and John generally travelled on a donkey. Word would be sent on from place to place, giving notice that they were coming and often they would be away for a month at a time.

On 17 December 1901 there was cause for much rejoicing at Mvumi as Rose gave birth to a daughter, Joan. John wrote 'Both mother and child are doing wonderfully well. Dr Baxter came over from Mamboya to attend her and we also have Mrs Rees with us. May God enable us to give back to him this his latest blessing on our married life.' Soon after Joan's birth Rose had some more children to look after. A German officer rescued five Wasandawi children who had been sold by their parents for food. The officer sent them to Rose to be cared for.

John was still a gardener and nurseryman by his early training, and he became famous for his fruit and vegetable garden at Mvumi which he was beginning to get established at this time. He dug wells and planted fruit trees of all kinds; orange, lemon, grapefruit, papaya, mango, and grape vines. In the shade of these he grew all sorts of vegetables.

Bishop Peel's next visit around his huge Diocese came in 1902 when he returned with his wife and daughter. They came to Mvumi and the Bishop remembered his visit of two years before. He wrote:

> In September 1902 Mr Briggs met my wife, my daughter and me on the same ridge and took us into a most comfortable and strongly-built house, with spacious verandah and double roof, one a flat roof of wood and mortar, one of thatch. The walls of the house were of stone and lime. He was indeed to be congratulated on having erected such a house, with such good doors and windows, at a cost of only £95, in the out-of-the-world Mvumi, as it used to be.
>
> Within two hundred yards was an excellent church-school, built tembe fashion, ie with the flat wood and mud roof so common in Chigogo. For accommodation of the teachers and their families a roomy tembe had been constructed. I was much

moved to give thanks to God. It was wonderful to see how He had set His blessing on the forward movement of the Mission.

We received a most warm welcome from Mr and Mrs Briggs .. It was quite refreshing to see little Joan, their baby, so sprightly though she was suffering from sore eyes and at times had much pain.

Soon an opportunity was afforded me of meeting and addressing the inquirers, of whom, to my surprise there were upwards of thirty on the register. With what power and freshness and clearness the Gospel story enters one's mind and heart, when the pleasant task is before one to make plain the whole state of human nature's degraded condition, and the whole prospect of the restoration of man to God's image and likeness in Christ. ... And what a grave responsibility it is to have to do this! Two of these inquirers, men, were publicly admitted by me to the class for catechumens. Since then they have been baptized. A branch of the Church of Christ has begun to sprout in Mvumi!

John and Bishop Peel walked still further west from Mvumi, to Kilimatindi, a distance of about two hundred miles there and back, which proved to Bishop Peel the scope for future work, if only they had the missionaries and their keep. His report continued:

Naturally, in the outlying portions of Mvumi, I noticed the warm recognition of Mr Briggs as of one belonging to the people. I will, however, only touch upon some events of the march after leaving Mwiticile. ... At Matumbiri we camped for a Sunday almost under an umbrageous and lofty ficus, whose great trunk shot up side by side with a fat and grotesque baobab. Not many, but some chief men, came from the tembes in the vicinity. They were very much pleased with Mr Briggs' sketch of Gospel truths, but shook their heads and said, 'we must hear often to understand.' Then they asked questions freely. Some of our porters, men who have been much with Mr and Mrs Briggs, but not even professed inquirers, began to explain the Gospel to these strangers at our tent-door. After listening to them, Mr Briggs allowed them to continue, because he noticed that they spoke so well to the point!

The great interest of our march, however, centred in a meeting with Masenha, who is a very big chief having as many as 100,000 persons in his sphere of jurisdiction. His territory is known as Unyangwira. Where to find him was the problem, for the stretch of country was great. ... The chain of providences was completed as we tramped up to the big tembe and were greeted by the influential chief, and led by him to the little stools at once procured for us. ... A pathetic scene followed. The chief, much attracted by Mr Briggs fluent Chigogo, fell to talking in good earnest. Again and again he insisted that he was correct in surmising that Briggs had interviewed him years ago on an occasion well remembered by him. He urged that he now wanted to talk on for two days, and was grieved when it was made clear to him that my tour admitted of only a brief delay at this end of Unyangwira. Pointing to a baobab tree of large proportions he said: 'That is my shauri [council] tree. Long ago, when I was a young warrior and used to rub red earth and oil over my body, a white man came to me and told me good words like yours, under that tree. He promised to come again, but he never did. You say that you will come again. No, you will be like that man.' Briggs was the while rapidly translating for my benefit. I put in words to the effect that I had specially asked the white man before him to visit him again. Would he build a school if we should be able to teach his people? Yes. Did he remember what the first white man taught him? Yes, he had not forgotten that good words were told him, but he was young then. It must have been dear Price who had sat under the baobab and had sought to bless Masenha and his warriors with the knowledge of God and the Lord Jesus Christ. A sinking sun brought us to our feet and compelled us to very reluctantly say farewell to the chief and to the respectful little crowd which had, in silence, witnessed our most interesting interview.

In December 1902 Bishop Peel called a conference at Mpwapwa. 'All the missionaries were able to be present except Mr and Mrs Wood, Mrs Doulton and Mrs Briggs and those on furlough. As many of the teachers as could be drawn from all the mission districts were joined with us in the profitable meetings held.' Even in those early days, when the native teachers were few and their education still quite basic they were

Travels with Bishop Peel

There is a stretch of swampy ground, half a mile or more across, through which the Mvumi track passes. After rain it means a walk knee-deep in soft mud! To this must be added an insignificant little stream which crosses the caravan path. In fine weather you descend into the bed, and step over the tiny rill. We saw it thus, and also otherwise. We numbered five Europeans and about forty porters and servants, a caravan escaping from mud and water and hurrying hopefully to a camp removed from all risks, when a stern halt was ordered. The little stream had become a river for men to swim in! Trees were numerous and lent themselves to bridging-arrangements. In a few hours a very shaky stand of poles and twigs was available in mid-stream. To it, and from it on the other side, it was possible for men to walk nearly breast-deep. With much trepidation I beheld my wife and daughter lifted, dragged and wobbled across. There were many slips and shouts, but no damage. Briggs and I were light-weights, and were carried easily, not having skirts. Mr Doulton required thirteen men to transport him.

Hyenas appear to thrive in Mvumi and Ibwijili [Buigiri], judging from their nocturnal parades. It was in Mvumi district that my porters once tried to protect their little stores of dried meat by sleeping on them. The hyenas waited until sleep was well established, and then extracted the morsels! The study of the habits of bugs of all sorts is forced upon you in Ibwijili after a good shower of rain. To have a meal in the evening by lamplight is hopeless in attempt, or disastrous in result, unless you place a large basin containing water in the middle of the table and put the lamp into it. Even with all the ingenious contrivances you may be able to command, your eating may prove uncomfortably emetic. One evening, when we were all on the alert, and saving our viands by spooning our afflictors into the basin, one black creature swooped into my tea. Mrs Doulton at once relieved me of the cup, threw away the tea, poured in hot water, and then gave me another cupful. I drank two mouthfuls and hurried off to my bedroom, and had to remain there some little time, not enjoying the emetic effects of the essence which had retained its strength so marvellously.

included in discussions and plans with the Bishop. Bishop Peel concludes his report with high praise for the missionaries of the mission in German East Africa 'a very high premium is set upon love, unity, concord, and prayer, as well as upon unselfish and laboriously faithful service. ... In my now somewhat long experience of missionary work I have never seen their devotion surpassed'.

In 1903 John and Rose suffered continual ill-health and Dr Baxter ordered them to return to England for a rest. They refused to go, since they said they were now better and many people were coming as inquirers. Since there was no-one else to take over the work they felt that the progress they were beginning to make would be lost should they leave. Between July and September the family spent 9 weeks in a tent again visiting the Kilimatindi region, travelling about encouraging the teachers. After such a long journey they were glad to get back to Mvumi again and 'received a most enthusiastic welcome home from the population on our hill.'

The beginning of 1904 saw the arrival of two new missionaries to Mvumi. The first was Miss Elizabeth Forsythe, aged 29, from Ireland, who wrote in her Annual Letter at the end of that year:

> I came on here ... on January 22nd, very glad indeed to find a home again after more than three months of wandering. Mr and

Miss Elizabeth Forsythe   Miss Violet Attlee
Courtesy CMS

Mrs Briggs made me feel quite happy and at home from the very first, and they have been exceedingly kind in every way.

The second was Miss Fendt, who later moved to Kongwa, a new station near Mpwapwa. Then, in June, Miss Violet Attlee came and joined them from Kongwa. She had been assigned to help the Rees there, but found that she was too nervous to sleep in a tent on her own so moved to Mvumi to join the other single ladies. Their first task was to learn Cigogo, while John was to build them a house for £100. That same year John reported

The year of 1904 was one of happy work, with real progress and also some extension. The usual services, school, and classes have been held on the station. My wife, as in previous years, managed the school, and she also held classes for women inquirers and catechumens. In addition to the Sunday services in the station we have for most of the year been able to hold services on Sunday afternoons at three different out-schools. In this we had valuable help from Andereya, a former teacher, who was dismissed for sin but who has since been restored to Church membership and is now working for us as a house-servant.

Our staff of native teachers, like last year, numbers four only, but we have this year had the help of two lads who have given themselves up for the Lord's work and been received by us as students. The small sum required for their maintenance has been met, in the case of [Nataneli] Cidosa by the Marienberg (Malvern) Bible-class, and the other one, Danyeli Sadala, by the church collections. These lads, as well as the teachers, have had regular instruction in reading, writing, New and Old Testament, geography, and arithmetic. My wife has undertaken this work.

School work and preaching is now being done in eleven centres (including the station). The number of people who can read is gradually increasing, and this year more books (New Testaments and Prayer-books and hymn-books) were sold than during any previous one. In August the Rev. H. Cole paid us a visit and three men, five women and five children were baptized.

There were questions being asked in Britain about the German East Africa mission and why it was not yet supporting its own evangelism, as compared with Uganda, where there was considerable growth. Bishop Peel in his report tries to counter this feeling with the bare facts:

> The bananas are not in East Africa what they are in Uganda and in the regions of the Lakes. Ugogo, in the absence of rain, is one vast red wilderness. Had we Uganda's growth of such staple food … we should have Uganda's support of preachers of the Gospel; for we have no lack of very friendly chiefs and sub-chiefs, and certainly we have most friendly people to deal with.

Finally Bishop Peel tried to explain the difficulties of asking people who were not Christians to support evangelism amongst them:

> In the early stage of the Christian teaching there may be much done for the messenger of the Gospel. The people, say, build him a house, provide him with milk and corn, and look after him in all ways. Instruction leads to knowledge of sin, and clearly points to abandonment of the sensual practices so rife, and separation from the much-dreaded medicine man. Men who prefer to go on in evil ways lose interest in 'the teacher'. They stop supplies! .. After the first few months the teacher has to hold fast to the people and be urgent in demands upon their attention when their interest has begun to flag and the new thing has ceased to attract. To this end the teacher must be paid from a source which does not fail him when his audiences, conscience stricken, dwindle away, and hard work, all against the collar has to be maintained for perhaps two years, or even longer, until one here and another there has been won to Christ. Then living witnesses to the Saviour of men boldly side with the villagers' patient but, for long unwelcome friend.

John wrote in his Annual Letter for 1904:

> On August 30th I left Mvumi with my wife and child for furlough. Owing to this the enormous Kilimatinde district has had to be left this year, which is a matter for real regret, as last year the people in many places seemed interested in the Gospel.

The Briggs family had stayed on longer than advised in order to keep the work in Mvumi going. Had they left sooner the new missionaries would not have been ready to be left alone. Even by the end of August, it must have seemed a bit risky leaving the new missionary ladies, who were still learning the language, to keep the work going. These ladies were in fact enabled to stay through the support and help of the teachers and people of the community at Mvumi.

For John, Rose and Joan this delay proved to be terrible. Rose was six months pregnant with their second child and so physically not in the best shape to undertake a long journey at what was becoming the hottest time of year. Their journey involved a long safari on foot down to the coast, and then travel by boat up the east coast of Africa and through the Suez Canal. The next part of the story is told most movingly in a letter written by John only a short time later:

> C/o Rev Thornton
> Cairo
> Wednesday 19th [October]

Dear Mr Baylis

I wired you yesterday the sad news of my dear wifes death. I will now give you details as well as I am able. You must please excuse a little incoherency as I seem in a sort of dream and can hardly realize things yet.

We left Mvumi Aug 29th and had a very good journey down country but during the twelve days we were at Dar es Salaam waiting for the boat we all had fever and my wife rather severely and I had to take her to the government hospital there. She seemed to get quite well by the time the ship arrived and was in her usual state of health until we got nearly through the Red Sea when she developed slight fever. I found it difficult to get her temperature quite down and the second day signs of blackwater fever appeared, slight at first, and we hoped as we were on the sea, in fact passing through the Canal, it would soon leave her. However the next day it was worse and what made things so very serious was her condition. She was pregnant and had been to about 6 months.

The next day, Monday, we got to Port Said and the port holes had to be closed on account of coaling. She nearly fainted from the heat but we got an electric fan and she revived somewhat. Just before the ship was leaving she was so bad that the doctor said I must take her ashore to hospital there as the risk from the motion of the boat was too great. She had been vomiting all night and was quite yellow. We were hurried off having no time even for packing. Our things were just done up in bundles and my wife was carried down in a mattress and put in a boat and we were sent off. The boatmen took us to the quarantine place where we were detained about 2 hours until two doctors had examined her. They were afraid of plague and yellow fever etc.It was awful for my poor wife. She just lay on a table on a sort of verandah and I feared she would die there. When we did get out I got a carriage and took her to the English hospital. I saw the doctor after waiting a little time but he said they were full up with men, had no womens ward, the private ward was already occupied by a lady, he could not possibly take her. She had been outside in the cab all this time. I begged him to do something for me and he said I had better go to the Egyptian (government) hospital. I drove there and at least I got her out of the awful sun and into a house. The doctor there (Dr Orme) was most kind. He did not wait for an order from British Consul which is necessary, but at once got her into a private ward and I drove off to the Consulate for the permit. I got this after paying a deposit of £20 and when I returned to my dear wife she just knew me and that was all. Soon after that she began to wander and by evening was quite unconscious. She never rallied and passed away at 3 o'clock the next morning (yesterday). The doctor said she suffered no pain as the poison had reached the main cells and there would be no feeling. This is my only comfort. It was terrible to see her lying unconscious, to know that she was dying and not be able to even take a last farewell. How I got through that night I do not know. I think having to care for the little one helped me. I had to keep up for her sake.

Canon Strange of Port Said was very kind to me and he arranged all about the funeral which took place yesterday at 2 pm. We buried her in the little cemetery by the side of the sea and then my desolation seemed complete.

I have to wait a fortnight for the next German steamer and I felt I could not bear the loneliness of Port Said. So Canon Strange wired to Mr Thornton here and they have most kindly taken me in for the time I have to wait. It is so nice for Joan to be where there is a lady. Poor little darling she keeps asking for her mother and she can't understand why she can't go to her.

I know God always does right so I rejoice that my darling is now in glory but it is hard to bear. I think it would have been easier had she been having all the comforts she needed during the illness but oh it was terrible to see her sufferings when she was being carried from place to place and I could do nothing to help her.

My ship (Kaiser) is due at Port Said Nov 3rd and I shall get off at Genoa and travel overland. I think we reach there about the 8th and I suppose I shall get to London about the 10th.

Sincerely Yours
John H Briggs

Rose was only 37 years old when she died, a heart breaking loss to John, Joan, and to all who knew her.

CHAPTER 3

Rebellion and Insecurity
1905–1909

John made a very hurried visit to England after Rose's death. In his letters he does not refer to her again, neither does he refer to their little daughter, Joan. He must have left Joan with relatives, probably with Rose's caring older brother Thomas, who was now a reporter in London and was married with a daughter. In the Annual Letter John wrote reporting on the year he did not mention this terrible event, either it was too painful or he considered it a private matter. Others wrote of the terrible loss, describing Rose as a 'missionary of outstanding capability and devotion', 'an inspiration' and as 'one of the most energetic and brightest workers of the Mission. By her wholehearted consecration to the work and kindness to everyone, she endeared herself to all who knew her.'

John made a three month trip to Germany to learn some language, in order to communicate better with the authorities back in German East Africa. He seemed to want to get back to work and to get on with life, in order to still the grief that must have pained him very badly. Not only had he lost his wife but he had also lost his partner in the work they had begun together. He didn't take the years leave that he was entitled to and returned early.

A letter from the Committee written to John on 9 May 1905, as he was about to return, said the following:

> The Committee know something of the mingled feelings with which you will now return to your work in German East Africa. They have felt for you and grieved with you in the loss of your

loved and honoured wife, a loss sorely intensified by the circumstances of her death and by the well recognized value of her own Missionary service. They do not forget that you must now bear the pain of separation from your little daughter. From their hearts they would assure you of their own true sympathy, and encourage you to rely to the utmost upon the sustaining sympathy and grace of Him of whom we are encouraged to believe that He is 'acquainted with grief' and 'able to succour'.

Imagine the reception John would have received from 'his people' on the hill this time; very possibly some may even have gone down to the coast to meet him. They would have reached out to him with heartfelt sympathy and gentle support, brought him gifts as is their custom on such occasions, and shared the grief for the woman that they too knew. It must have been hard for him to return alone to the home that they had made together but no doubt he also wanted to build on the work that they had started together.

John had only a short time at Mvumi before he turned back down to the coast to escort the Bishop up. Bishop Peel seems to have kept John with him for a large part of this extended visit, no doubt with the intention of keeping him close and in good company as much as possible, so as to keep loneliness and sadness at bay. Pictures of John at this time show a man barely recognisable, a gaunt figure hidden behind an enormous beard. Unfortunately none of these pictures are of sufficient quality to reproduce.

Back in 1902 Bishop Peel had chosen the site for a new mission building – a 'health resort' or sanatorium was sorely needed as at that time there were already 10 missionary graves in the Mpwapwa area. Bishop Peel described the occasion:

The entrancing summits of the Kiboriani group of mountains were selected as the place of trial. ... [we] undertook the pleasant climb and scramble, ending in a three nights' camp in most bracing air and gladdening surroundings. We literally inspected every available place, walking miles and miles without fatigue. Finally Mrs Peel turned the first sod of the ground where the house was to be, after our earnest prayer to God for His blessing, just 300 feet below the highest peak, on a sheltered table land spur which dived down into depths promising some struggling walks in days to come. There, perhaps 6,100 feet above sea-level, the sanatorium stands almost finished as I write.

The chosen site was in the mountain range between Kongwa and Mpwapwa.. The missionaries were constantly battling with fatigue and fever, but up on the heights of Kiboriani they would be away from mosquitoes and heat, they would be able to rest and regain their strength. T. B. R. Westgate, a Canadian CMS missionary who had arrived in 1902, had been given the task of building it. Bishop Peel wrote to the Committee in London on 2 August 1905 from Kongwa.

> I have come today from Kiboriani where, in the Sanatorium (5,600 feet above sea level) so well constructed by Mr Westgate, nineteen of us were housed for 'Conference' . . . and for a little bit of African Keswick. . . . We have all parted feeling that the season has been a blessed one for spirits, souls and bodies. The air is very bracing, the scenery soul-touching, the house comfortable and the place quite ideal for conferences and missionary reunions.

Kiboriani quickly became a central and essential part of missionary life. The air so high up is always cool in the shade, and can even be distinctly cold, but the sun can still be hot. The view from the sanatorium is spectacular, looking to the north across the plains, and surrounded on other sides by mountain peaks. Westgate did indeed build well and the remains of the building are still there today. Each room had a fireplace with a beautiful stone hearth, and opened onto one of the long verandahs front and back. The central room was a very big room in which all could meet for meals, conferences and general encouragement. Nearly a hundred years later I found a rose growing just beside the steps and I wondered who planted it.

After passing their first Cigogo examination in July Misses Attlee, Fendt and Forsythe heard that they were assigned to continue working at Mvumi 'much to our joy' wrote Elizabeth Forsythe.

Only weeks later the whole country was thrown into a state of confusion by the Maji Maji Rebellion. Sparked by the German imposition of a tax, medicine men incited the tribes to rebel against the white man and drive him out by giving people maji-maji (magic waters) to drink. This magic water was said to make them impervious to bullets. Bishop Peel got news of it whilst at Mvumi in early September. The rebellion had started in the south-east corner of German East Africa, and quickly spread up the coast and eastern highlands, making the route to the coast unsafe. If the Wahehe joined the rebellion then Ugogo would also be likely to be raided, and the mission houses would be unsafe because at that time they were all thatched with grass which could easily be set alight. The missionaries carried on working, and waited for news. In October, however, the chief of Idifu, near Mvumi, became disaffected with the Germans and drank the maji-maji, and so it was necessary to call Miss Atlee and Miss Fendt to Kongwa and Miss Forsythe to Kiboriani.

The unrest continued to build however, and Bishop Peel wrote

At Kongwa on Tuesday 14th [November] Mr and Mrs Rees welcomed us three fugitives into their home [John, Bishop Peel and his daughter Agneta]. We gave ourselves to enjoy relief from such strain and looked forward to some days of opportunity to go on with life's business. On Wednesday night about 9 pm we were all startled to hear that the Wabinga were within 25 miles of us, burning villages and killing people. Instead of going to bed we worked all night, packing up the goods of Mr and Mrs Rees. While we were thus engaged we heard the war cry going the round of Kongwa. ... On Thursday we joined all the rest of the staff in the Sanatorium, a building with a lime and sand roof in which we could make a good stand against the enemy.

The Sanatorium became an asylum for all the missionaries in the district from November 1905. They were not in danger from the tribes amongst whom they were known and had worked, but had the rebels reached Kiboriani they would probably not have been interested in differentiating between missionaries and German occupiers. There were German soldiers at the fort in Mpwapwa who could be called on if necessary; the ladies made 900 sandbags to keep out poisoned arrows and the men built a stockade around the house in case the rebels reached it. Because of concerns for safety, no one was able to go far from the house, but Westgate made a tennis court and that provided some diversion. The tennis court can still be seen to the south east of the Sanatorium, next to the remains of the old church; it has a beautiful retaining wall to create the necessary level ground on a mountain top. The local Wagogo people kept them informed of the rebel movements throughout. In the middle of all this Rita Westgate gave birth to a daughter.

The siege lasted several months, and it was only in the second half of 1906 that the missionaries could return to their stations. They had used their time doing translation work; John translated more hymns into Cigogo. He returned to Mvumi in May, and had considerable building work to do, since there had been exceptionally heavy rains while they were at Kiboriani and the mission buildings were in the traditional style with flat mud roofs, meaning that they suffered badly in heavy rain. After the experience of the Maji-Maji rebellion, the missionaries decided that the traditional roofs should be replaced with iron roofs and that floors should be cemented (should they get the money from London) for greater security and longevity of buildings. When Bishop Peel finally left to return to Mombasa in mid-1906, John escorted him to the coast, a round trip of hundreds of miles.

Misses Attlee, Fendt and Forsythe remained at Kongwa until all signs of the rebellion had disappeared, Miss Fendt then remained at Kongwa and Misses Attlee and Forsythe returned to Mvumi. Even so it was reported at the end of the year that the ladies had managed to open a new higher grade school at Mvumi that year, for those who had passed through the elementary school. Through these schools and the 'on the job' teaching of teachers the capacity of the mission was growing very slowly. These teachers were the earliest native church leaders and even at this early stage John formed a church council, seeking to involve them in the decisions that were made.

The new year of 1907 saw a new comfort for John, as he wrote to the Committee in January to inform them of his engagement to Violet Attlee, and expressing the hope that the British author-

ities would agree to their being married in Mpwapwa by a
German officer.

During the week beginning 7 April 1907 Mvumi saw its first
evangelistic mission. John wrote:

> The effort was to try and bring to a decision the large numbers
> who attend Sunday services, but in every other respect remain
> as Heathen. God was present with us at all the meetings and
> manifested His power. At the close of the last meeting seventy-
> six men and women stood up and before all the congregation
> expressed their determination to be Christians. The following
> Sunday they were publicly admitted into the inquirers' class.
> Since then a few others have also joined who were prevented by
> various causes from attending that last meeting, making in all
> over eighty inquirers as a result of this mission.

Miss Forsythe was now in charge of the dispensary, which was
considered a very important part of the work, and always busy.
In the first seven months of 1907 the attendances numbered
5950, an average of maybe 30 people per day. Physical sickness
often brought people into contact with the mission where
nothing else would. If the local medicine man had not been able
to cure somebody, as a last resort they came to the mission. If
they were then healed, it was a major factor in slowly breaking
the power of the medicine man, a power that was usually based
on fear and superstition rather than the Christian message of
love and reconciliation. The missionaries saw so much needless
death and suffering that it was often both heartbreaking and
frustrating. It was felt, even in 1907, that the mission in Ugogo
really needed a doctor, since there were many difficult cases
about which untrained people could do nothing, and so the
people returned to the medicine man again.

Interest in the mission was growing, perhaps in part this was
because the defeat of the Maji-Maji rebellion was understood by
people to be a defeat for the power of the medicine man. John
reported:

> It is no platitude to say that everywhere is open to us as perhaps
> never before. The chiefs immediately around are eager for us to

go to their particular countries and teach them to read. Some, seeing the fewness of our numbers, and despairing of many visits from us, have sent lads to live near or with us to be taught. The country is certainly waking up in the matter of education and this gives us our opportunity. ... In fact when a man gets so far emancipated from the trammels of ancient custom as to want the new learning, he is generally open in his mind and ready to go the whole way. It is safe to say that if the Church of God does not rise to this opportunity, in a few years it will have passed, never perhaps to come again. Coast influence is coming in like a flood, with a railway almost at our doors, and traders everywhere.

On the continuation of the higher grade school he wrote:

We are very much handicapped having no suitable buildings. The church is also school and in this way we manage for the elementary stage. When we started this higher grade we were able to make use of a little classroom for the purpose, though it proved too small for over thirty pupils. This is now in ruins, and for the past year we have had to do what we could in a store room. ... Of course everything like desks or proper seats is unknown with us. They just have to manage for their writing with a board on the knee.

On 27 August 1907 John and Violet, in the company of the Westgates, left for the coast. The Westgates were going on leave and they travelled together as far as Mombasa, where John and Violet were married in the Cathedral by Bishop Peel on 30 September 1907. John was now a mature 39 years old, and Violet was 36. Another honeymoon 'march' followed, with the usual arduous return journey to make, travelling on foot from the coast. The heat and exhaustion caused Mrs Briggs to have a miscarriage, when they were some way on their journey. John reported:

We had to make a long stay at the place where it happened and again after we got to Berega where Mr and Mrs Deekes were most kind to us – Dr Baxter made a forced march and came to our help at Mto wa Mawe.

They went to Kiboriani for Mrs Briggs to recover and were still there in December, when they were joined by Bishop Peel and a gathering of the missionaries for a conference. The main subject for discussion was the question that still loomed over them, the question of handing over the mission to another society. Naturally all argued against such a proposal. John and Violet stayed at Kiboriani until Violet was fully recovered in the New Year, being away from Mvumi for four months in order to be married.

In July of 1908 Nataneli Chidosa and Elia Muyohi passed their probationers exams, which meant that they were then able to teach at a higher level. In this year the Mvumi District Out Schools increased from 8 to 14, though unfortunately there is no record found of where these were. However it is recorded that they were well established and operating effectively, highly valued by the people. A shortage of workers, both missionary and native, was all that limited the growth of the work at this time. Missionaries were few in number because London continued to feel that the British mission operating in German territory had an uncertain future. The number of native teachers was small because the work was still in its early days. Only a few people were both quick to take the words spoken, allowing God to change their lives, and also quick of mind to learn to read and write.

Apart from Nataneli and Elia, who else was likely to have been assisting at this time? People like Andreya Lungwa (though still not restored to full status), Paulo Cidinda, Lazaro Hembokamu, Benyamini Mulugu, Simeyoni Camulomo, Danyeli Sadala, Yohana Cagwa, Musa Muhumha, Dawudi Citema, Nehemiya Malima, Noha Lukuna, Maruko Malima and possibly others not identified. The importance of these teachers should never be underestimated, and to this day their names are known in the area. They took the faith that they received, the stories they were told and the words that they read, and interpreted them in many different villages in Ugogo. They were the foot soldiers that made the army, the farmers planting and tending the seeds, often walking hours a day to teach a class to read, teach a simple Bible story and a song and return home to Mvumi. Nataneli later recalled that his first experience of teaching was with Benyamini

Mulugu at Handali and then he went on a two month tour with Lazaro Hembokamu, making a big circuit and visiting places for a one or two week stay. When they returned another teacher went, and so on; they would take it in turns to be on the road. Nataneli did this journey many times. Without such people the work could not have grown, there would have been no harvest. John later wrote: 'These African evangelists were fine fellows, and it was an inspiration to see them starting off on a Monday morning for their long tramp, with reading sheets from which to teach.'

The growth of the work of teaching combined with the understaffing of the mission became a more and more pressing

problem. The greater the number of people able to teach, the more work necessarily fell upon the missionary for their continuing education, to fit them for the job. The teachers at Mvumi lived close by, so that they could regularly receive instruction to improve their own knowledge and under-

Teaching from the cloth
Courtesy Banks family

standing. They needed to be supplied with materials to teach with, such as 'the cloth', still remembered by older people in the area. This was a piece of unbleached calico with letters and syllables painted on in pen and ink, and then a deep hem sewn for a stick, so that the sheet could be suspended from a hut or a tree. The preparation of such cloths was very laborious and as the school work increased it was nearly impossible to keep up supply.

Miss Forsythe went on leave in August, leaving John and Violet at Mvumi. While she was away she did a course of midwifery at Battersea in London. Only shortly after her departure John wrote back to London with some sad news:

My wife gave birth to a son (of course premature) on November 30th. He lived one day and I baptised him by the name of Henry Guy. He now lies in our little cemetery here and is a very precious link in the chain that binds Mvumi very closely to our hearts.

A present day reminder of the sorrow felt at this loss is that in the little cemetery on the east side of the hill, which was used for burials by the first Christians, Henry Guy's grave was the only one marked with a beautiful cross inscribed with his name.

The railway being built up from the coast by the Germans now reached as far as Mpwapwa, meaning that such useful items as iron roofing sheets and cement were more accessible and affordable since they didn't have to be carried from the coast on someone's head. John was always one to improve the material surroundings when he could, and so 'at Mvumi the mission-house and all the outbuildings are in thorough repair. Recent improvements afford excellent accommodation for the mission staff.'

There were many demands on the missionary's time, it being shared between practical issues such as building, together with teaching, taking services, visiting, teaching the teachers, and travelling. This meant that certain other important tasks such as translation always went to the bottom of the priority list. The New Testament, a prayer book and hymn book had already been translated into Chigogo, but these needed amending since there were printers errors and the translation of the Old Testament still had a long way to go. The plea was always to send more people out, but there was little response. The longing for a doctor continued.

The scope and possibilities for employment of medical skill are boundless: the results achieved, insignificant. Once more we appeal, and we trust not in vain, for a properly equipped Medical Mission, to break down the power of the Medicine man and to alleviate the sufferings of the hundreds of thousands of Wagogo.

Bishop Peel wrote to the Committee in London, despairing that they were not supporting the work as it deserved.

All preaching is accompanied by an effort to teach people to read so they may have the help of God's word. I am amazed at the number who now can read and more so when I know the difficulties. People are coming several hours walk, because they are not able to get sufficient teaching in their homes they attend the station church. Your heart would have been grieved and burdened to look upon the many places where people are no longer hostile but willing to listen for whom we can afford no teacher. A very great change has come over the people who have felt the influence of the CMS staff in Ugogo ... but through our weakened European staff and fewness of African teachers we cannot take advantage of it, but I believe that God will care.

Westgate visited briefly at Christmas 1908, being an ordained man he was able to give Holy Communion. He also baptised Asani Ndigana, Isaya Cilongani and his son Haroni, and Sila Njamasi and his son Luka. Violet wrote about it in a very descriptive letter:

We had three very interesting adults baptised – three men who have been very decided heathen all their lives and two of whom have given up their extra wives and settled down with one only, to live Christian lives. These two also brought their youngest children to be baptised. Their wives are not yet Christians but they are being taught and we hope they will be baptised before very long. The women are particularly hard to teach, as they have so much work to do and their <u>brains</u> are not accustomed to working. Sometimes after making them repeat something very simple, when asked the question which practically tells them the answer which they have just been repeating, they will look quite surprised and ask 'How should we know?' However I am glad to say they are not all like this and some can read and write quite nicely, and just lately several have begun to make a very special effort, and have bought books and their husbands are helping them in their spare time at their villages. The outschool work is most encouraging – we have good numbers almost always now, and several have their own New Testaments and are reading them, and tell us when they come here that they can see for themselves now that the words we tell them are true.

Violet goes on to describe a Sunday afternoon service at Itumbi (the area just west of Mvumi hill) where 14 people were admitted as inquirers. The service was taken by Andereya (Lungwa) who she describes as 'a most earnest Christian ... and is most keen on doing any voluntary work that he can'. She goes on

> At Mazengo's, the big chief of this country, they have been waking up lately. The three boys from there are still here and can all read and write and do simple arithmetic. One has brought his wife here and they are settled in a house of their own, the other two are not married and are still in our boy's house. ... They were admitted as catechumens [for baptism] a few Sundays ago and are I believe real Christians. We hope they will go back home sometime to be a real power amongst the people in their own district.

Chief Mazengo was the young chief of the Mvumi district, and had a very significant influence on the development of the mission and on his people. He and John established a friendship of mutual respect and affection that spanned across decades. Mazengo was not prepared to undertake instruction himself, but he was very happy for members of his village to take the opportunity.

Finally Violet reports:

> One of the teachers, Lazaro [Hembokamu] has school everyday now in the afternoon for the Christian children etc; we gave them a little examination the other day and found they were really getting on very well. They learn the three 'rs' and geography and are taught the commandments, catechism etc thoroughly.

The German District Officer of the time, Sperling, visited Mvumi and said that he wanted the sons of every chief to learn to read and write. This was an opportunity for the Mission to have more influence amongst the future leaders but staff were so few that it was impossible for them to do more than they were already doing.

In February 1909 Rose's companion in those early days, Ellen Doulton, died of peritonitis at her home in Kongwa.. Her last words were 'I am tired, let me go'. Ernest Doulton wrote to

London to inform them of this sad news, saying 'may this further thinning of our ranks be a loud call to send forth more labourers.'

At about the same time there was a Pan-Anglican Thank offering (an offering given across the whole Anglican church) and Bishop Peel submitted a scheme of Education in a bid for some of the money. He was granted £4,000. Good news at last.

Naturally there was concern for Violet's health, which was not so good after the birth and early death of their son. With her highly-strung nature she was still dependent on close company to calm her nerves. She had been in East Africa since 1903 and it was felt that John and Violet should return to England for a rest. However she was not really fit enough to travel, and Miss Forsythe was still away which would mean leaving Mvumi without a missionary, something they were reluctant to do. They stayed on until the end of August 1909, and then it was not too long before Miss Forsythe returned in November.

As soon as Miss Forsythe did arrive she had the assistance of a new 29 year old missionary woman from Australia, Miss Effie Jackson. Miss Jackson had been waiting to leave Australia for some time, but CMS Australia did not have the money to send her until 1909 and she had no private means. Effie Jackson had finished her schooling and then been occupied with domestic duties – presumably at home – until she entered the Deaconess Institute as a probationer deaconess. It was while she was in training that she applied to CMS. The Superintendent wrote to CMS about her as follows:

> I can speak very highly of Miss Jackson. Her personal piety is deep and sincere and she has a clear grasp of Christian doctrine. She has obtained a 1st class pass at the recent exam by Canon Jones. Her work in the slums of St Andrews Cathedral has given me ample opportunity to prove that her zeal for souls is born of Him, and God has let me observe signs and tokens that He has blessed her work, which has largely been among the drunken and fallen. Her education has been a good plain one, and she has mental ability being studious and capable of reasoning out problems. Her influence, while being a very quiet one in the Home, has been a very marked one. Her standard is a high one. I write

more fully of her because I fear her reserve may prevent her excellent character being discerned.

Miss Effie Jackson
Courtesy CMS Australia

On Miss Jackson's arrival at the end of 1909 her first task, as you will now know, was to learn Swahili and Chigogo.

By the end of 1909 things were looking a bit brighter. Miss Jackson had arrived with two other new recruits to the region, Rev. Green and Miss Thwaites. Andrea Lungwa and a teacher from Kongwa were helping with the revised translations of the entire New Testament. At last there was the prospect of progress once again.

John, reporting from England for the year of 1909, wrote that the Christians had rebuilt the Church and enlarged it, complete with a beaten lime and sand floor.

> This building is in conformity with the native style of architecture and of the usual materials employed in their house building and so will only last a limited time, but for the present it provides a commodious and comfortable place for services and school. About 500 people can crowd into it, and we often have it full.

Other building developments that took place that year were a new waiting room on the dispensary and a new sick ward for a few to be admitted when absolutely necessary.

There was, as ever, sad news as well, perhaps felt all the more keenly by John since the death of his own son Henry.

> I am sorry to say we have lost, through death, a great many of the babies who were baptised. Our people have yet to learn the proper way to rear children. They are skilful in bringing up their calves, kids etc but they do not know the way to feed young babies. It is nice to feel that these little ones have been taken home to the Fathers house before the blight of sin can touch them and that the Church triumphant is necessary but we would like to see the Church militant benefit more from this young life which ought to be growing up amongst us.

It is interesting that he talks of 'our people' where many other missionaries talk of 'the people' or 'the natives'. He strongly identifies himself with them. His seemingly unkind observations of child caring skills are not necessarily unfair; it was estimated that child mortality in the first quarter of the century amongst the Wagogo was about 80%.

A final problem, and rather a different one to the present day church: 'Male adult baptisms are greatly in excess of female and we are already feeling the difficulty when our Christian men want to marry. There is also a lower grade of Christian life.'

The missionaries on the field were keen to get their hands on some of the Pan-Anglican money that Bishop Peel had been granted. They proposed building four schools, one in Mamboya, one in Kongwa, one in Mvumi, and one in Buigiri (between Kongwa and Mvumi). The teaching was very important but also time consuming. They had run out of Chigogo New Testaments for the students but Doulton didn't feel he could print any more until the translation was revised. He felt it would take himself and Westgate a whole eight months to complete the revision. Progress seemed more than an uphill struggle; without more help it seemed impossible.

CHAPTER 4

A Ripening Harvest, Loss in War 1910–1918

The year of 1910 saw the new German railway reach Buigiri, completely changing travel in the country ever after. John put it this way: 'much of the romance of African travel disappeared with the advent of the iron horse', though he did admit it was kind of useful. In January John wrote to the Committee requesting that he spend extra time in England to prepare for ordination.

> I have felt ever since I have been at Mvumi that my usefulness would be increased if I were in Holy Orders and now that the Church there is growing so rapidly it has been more and more borne in upon me that the district needs a clergyman.

Whilst on leave John typed up the Chigogo translation of Exodus and Numbers which he had revised with Doulton. He then had to spend time getting them ready for printing by the British and Foreign Bible Society and checking on them at every stage. This took about six months, and to prepare for Holy Orders he needed to do reading and study (including Greek and Latin) to pass Bishop Peels exam for ordination. He knew this would be impossible to do once back at Mvumi. The Briggs were allowed to stay, and one factor affecting this was that Andereya Lungwa was about to be re-employed as a teacher, so Miss Forsythe and the new Miss Jackson would have his very able help. Andereya must have proved himself absolutely, since it had been previously stated that after his breaking the seventh commandment (adultery) in 1901 he could never be reinstated as a teacher.

There were poor harvests in June of 1910 and these were followed at the end of the year with an invasion of army worms and drought, so that by the beginning of 1911 there was considerable famine. Despite these changes and hardships there was a remarkable awakening to the Christian faith at this time. Doulton wrote about a service in Mvumi that he took where 500 were present and, of these, 130 enrolled for teaching. In the year of 1911 a total of 733 people were admitted for instruction. Westgate also reported on the Mvumi district after a visit in March. With John still away, the eight native teachers had made strenuous efforts to keep up with the demand for teaching and were officially commended for their faithfulness; eight chiefs had built churches and were waiting for a teacher, even Mazengo himself had enrolled as an enquirer.

At the end of 1910 Miss Forsythe wrote that although she had been back for a whole year, she had been ill with malarial fever for half that year. Miss Jackson had been busy learning Swahili, so that they had done little travel around the district. Their time was taken up at Mvumi keeping things going and helping the teachers in their study. She reports that there were a lot of children coming daily to school for the scripture lesson. She was teaching them 100 texts to learn by heart, each with a simple explanation. Miss Forsythe's class included 26 sons and nephews of chiefs, mostly from unreached districts.

This growth in the work is illustrated by a descriptive passage from the Mombasa Diocesan Magazine.

The unprecedented extension which characterized the year was most marked in the Mvumi district. Sunday after Sunday people stood up in church, from eight or nine to more than one hundred at a time, publicly renouncing Heathenism, and confessing their wish to learn more about the Saviour. At a place called Mima, whence messengers had often been received asking for teachers, the chief addressed Bishop Peel, as follows: 'I am old ... many of us are old. We cannot hope to learn to read the Book. But there are many young ones whom you can teach. They can learn to read, but we all want to know the words. We all want to believe in the God you tell us about.' A great deal of the success which was met with was due, under God, to the faithful work of the African agents.

On the 29 March 1911 a formal agreement was made in Mpwapwa between the German East African Government in Dar, represented by Sperling (the officer at Mpwapwa), and CMS represented by Doulton who was Secretary of the Mission at the time. CMS purchased land at Buigiri, Berega, Mamboya, Nyangala, Mvumi (36.5 hectares), Kisokwe, and Kiboriani; a total of 251.3 hectares for 440 Rupees, equivalent to 80 German Heller. As far as Mvumi was concerned this agreement, together with the stones laid out as markers on the land, was the only legal basis of ownership of property until 1999 when the Tanzanian Government remarked it.

John and Violet returned to Mvumi in June of 1911, and for Mvumi mission this was the start of a significant era. For the next twenty years the team of missionaries stationed at Mvumi would revolve around these people; Miss Forsythe now well-established and well-known, in charge of the dispensary; Miss Jackson now finding her feet with the language and a teacher through and through; Violet and John, entering his prime as a man who knew what he was doing, vigorous and practical, respected and even awed, a generous provider, a kind of tribal chief whose heart was wholly devoted to proclaiming God's words of life and hope to the Wagogo, and to nurturing the seedling church just as he nurtured his own productive garden.

On John's return he and Westgate were immediately thrown into negotiations with the Roman Catholics. The Mvumi district was an area of 5,000 square miles into which the Catholics had been encroaching, and now wanted to make a new agreement. Reluctantly, John and Westgate agreed to cut the district:

> It was thought the wisest policy on our part, considering the meagreness of our resources as well as the financial condition of the society. It has caused us all very much pain indeed to relinquish even as much territory as we have felt obliged to do.

While together John and Westgate spent some time engaged in the translation of the Thirty Nine Articles, a sign that the native churchmanship was developing.

The agreement with the Catholics did not end the conflict, the

Catholics continued to be quite aggressive in their methods of evangelism, sometimes using force to make people choose them.[†] This, together with the growing desire of the people to learn, forced a change in the way the Mvumi mission was organized which John described in a booklet, entitled 'In the East Africa War Zone' which he wrote a few years later. All the quotes in this chapter marked with an asterisk* are taken from this publication.

> The only thing to do was to open out-stations at the most promis-
> ing centres and let the teachers live out there among the people.
> For this plan a larger native staff was necessary, but an appeal to
> the Christian congregations provided the men.*

This can be seen in the records: 1911 was the start of an Exodus from Mvumi, when many of the first Christians went to live in more distant places. John continued the account:

> The men were rather lacking in adequate training, there being no
> institution which could supply this in the Mission. On this
> account it was somewhat in fear and trembling that they were
> sent out to live for long periods away from the mission station and
> with all the cares of an out-station on their shoulders. The
> success, however, of this new act of faith was from the first
> assured. The very isolation of the teachers cast them more upon
> God, and His strength was made perfect in their weakness. The
> people too were overjoyed at having their own teachers living
> among them.*

Who were these people? Paulo Cidinda went to Handali; Lazaro Hembokamu went to Mpunguzi; Benyamini Mulugu went to Chief Mazengo's at Makulu; Nehemiya Malima went to Witicila as did Yoshuwa Mwaluko; Elieza Mhungwe went to Manhum-bulu. But there were many many more who went, to as many as thirty-five different places and some of these places were a good number of days journey away. It should be remembered that their wives would have been equally tested having to set up home

---

[†] For more on this see E Knox, *Signal on the Mountain* ch 21: Roman Catholic Incursion.

in a new and strange place. The scale of growth was now beyond the capacity of John alone to act as overseer of the work. John took Mika Muloli on a few of his camping trips visiting teachers in out-schools and then Mika started to undertake these journeys on his own.

The missionaries felt very strongly that there should be a training institution for these teachers to be able to go to for further training, now that it was impossible to do the training on the job. They also felt that it was time to ordain five well-tried teachers as deacons; these were Andereya Ndulesi (this must be Andereya Lungwa) of Mvumi, Yohana of Buigiri, Andereya Mwaka of Kissokwe, Eliyeza of Kongwa, Musa of Berega, and recommended them to Bishop Peel with the suggestion that they should have titles carrying 15 Rupees per month, rising to 20 Rupees when priested.

Miss Jackson managed to pass her language exams. She had much to write about in her Annual Letter for 1911.

> I have been able to help every day with the day school and during the later months have undertaken it altogether. We are looking forward to soon having a good and well furnished building. At present we use the church, a long low building of poles plastered with mud, with a thick earth roof and each side a row of porthole like windows. It is low because of the difficulty of getting long poles – in fact any poles at all – in this district of baobab trees and thorn bushes. The interior is whitewashed, the roof is supported by rows of poles, the floor is lime and sand. ... The scholars on the roll number 517. During the last month the attendance has been between 200 and 300 every day. Men, women and children come to learn the three R's, the children perhaps in the majority. ... During the last months there have been more women and girls than men and boys, a matter for rejoicing, as comparatively few women have sought the teaching in the past, and the many Christian young men have difficulty in finding Christian wives. Of course our first aim is to teach them to read, that they may read the word of God for themselves. They begin with the syllables printed on a sheet hung on the wall. They all shout them together after the teacher, and with three classes going on at once school is rather a noisy place. As soon as they have mastered the syllables, which is very difficult work for many of them, they start with a

first reading book. When they have really managed to read this, they enter the Testament Class. The majority have their own books and you may see them sitting about reading out of school hours.

These lessons went hand in hand with preparation for baptism since 'our rule is that they shall be able to read the New Testament, and have a grasp of the Truths connected with the birth, death and resurrection of our Lord, before they are baptised.'

Miss Jackson had considerable praise for the head teacher, who must have been Andereya Lungwa:

Our head teacher is invaluable. He has the power of controlling the crowd, and a good natured way of exacting obedience which so few of his companions have. This, combined with a lack of self-seeking, a willingness to do whatever comes to his hand, no matter how menial and an ever watchful readiness to seize opportunities of witnessing for his Master and urging His claims, must have a far-reaching influence.

The Pan Anglican Thankoffering finally filtered through the system, and there was £950 to build three schools (Mvumi, Buigiri and Berega). Even then, it took a while to put into action. It was 1912 before John reported that he had spent a third of his time that year building the school at Mvumi, a building with stone walls and a corrugated iron roof, and by the end of October it was nearly finished. He had had to be directly involved because the only way to keep within budget was by close supervision and by doing some of the skilled labour himself. Nearly twenty years after he arrived in Kisokwe and started building, it was still important to him to make sure something was really well built. Naturally, this building still stands; it has had many other uses in the intervening years, German garrison, doctor's house, and most recently a school cookhouse.

Local people say that this schoolroom was built by the Germans but there is no written record of such a thing; the records all refer to the Pan-Anglican money, and John reports building it with his own hands. Perhaps this association of the schoolroom with the Germans has developed because it was being built at the time that the German authorities ordered chiefs' sons to be educated. The chiefs could choose where; John wrote 'it is only a merited testimony to the popularity of our Mission to find that almost all in the vicinity of Buigiri and Mvumi have made application to us.'

Miss Jackson's Annual Report for 1912 mentioned what seems to be the first female teacher appointed: 'she is very bright and intelligent.' She described the way school had developed in Mvumi that year.

> We are looking forward to occupying the Pan-Anglican Thank offering building, which is now nearing completion. The general Day School is held only in the afternoon, but special school is held in the morning for the sons of chiefs, who are living at Mvumi that they may be educated, also for pupil teachers. ... Our headteacher is a great stand-by, his influence is always for the best in everything connected with the school.

Arrangements with the Roman Catholics broke down, leaving the whole of Ugogo open to both missions. The Roman Catholics had placed their agents beside those of CMS, 'with the object of making it impossible for our men to remain ... although the churches and people at whose request we occupied the places still prefer us.'

Applications for teachers increased so much that it seemed impossible to entertain any more. John told

> It was no uncommon thing for the missionary, awakened early in the morning by voices outside on the veranda, to find when he got up that it was a party of Africans from some distant place – perhaps fifty or even a hundred miles away – who had come to see him and beg for a teacher to go back with them and live in their country and teach them 'the words'. Such groups of people would stay with the teachers and some of the Christians at the station and use all their eloquence to persuade one to return with them; and bitter was their disappointment when perhaps they had to return home without one. All this made a great impression on the native Church, until there was a corresponding revival in it in regard to offers of service. Men began to offer in greater numbers than one had even dared to hope for a year before.*

In 1912 these people were amongst those who responded to that call: Petero Cisota went to Muhalala; Danyeli Munyaweha went to Mima; Tadayo Malecera went to Makangwa; Lazaro Musonga went to Ciwona; Yeremiya Ndunhyila went to Nhumbika; Yosiya Mugonhwa went to Cinugulu; Petero Mukwayi went to Mbijili; Musa Mabenanga went to Muhalala; Andereya Mupilimi went to Nghambala.

There was real growth too in the spiritual life of the Christians. John described it:

> The prayers of the Christians became more real as they saw God's workings in the heart of the heathen around. Bible-reading increased and the sales of the Scriptures went up. There was also a decrease in the number of those who fell into gross sin, as they came to know and trust in God's power to keep as well as to save. This change in the inner man produced greater carefulness in outer things, and the people became more particular about matters of dress ... personal cleanliness. Sunday was better observed and became the recognized day for public worship, the adherents of the Mission gathering in great numbers in the churches, which were sometimes crowded out. ... The Church had become a missionary church.*

Bishop Peel, arriving for a visit in September 1913, began to see what John had seen for a long time. That the effectiveness of the Church to minister was severely limited by the fewness of the number of ordained ministers. Westgate had walked 100 miles in recent times, just to administer Holy Communion. As the weight of work increased this happened less and less. Bishop Peel saw that it not only put a great strain on the ordained men but also limited the ministry of the church:

> Briggs, Doulton and Deekes have approached me touching ordinations for service in this diocese. ... Archdeacon Rees has begged me to ordain the three Deacon and Priest on Ordination Sunday fixed for November 23rd. God willing I have told the men concerned that I am willing, and shall be thankful to do so.

Left to right back row: Rev. King, Rev. John Briggs, Rev. Wright with Rev. Verbi behind (both of Mombasa), Rev. Westgate, Rev. David Deekes
Front row: Rev. Rees, Bishop Peel, Rev. Ernest Doulton
Courtesy Banks Family

The condition that the Bishop gave was that they carefully study all the subjects for the Priests exam and to make the Greek New Testament a constant study! So Deekes, Briggs and Doulton were all ordained deacon on 16th November 1913 and priested on 23rd November, in the church at Kiboriani by Bishop Peel. A recent arrival, King, was priested at the same time. Peel also formed Ugogo into an Archdeaconry of which Rees was the first Archdeacon. In the review of the year it was written 'In nothing has God given clearer guidance or shown his Fatherly care more for the tender stage through which our work is passing than by these ordinations. They are both buttress and pillar to it.'

Westgate had just returned from Canada before these ordinations, where he had raised the money to build a college at Kongwa for training church teachers and ministers. He had returned for just one year without his wife and family in order to complete this task, before starting a new work as a missionary to the native people of Canada. He set to work, building in stone and lime, an elegant and stately two storey building that still

The first students at Kongwa.
Left to right back row: Paulo Chidinda, Yusufu of Berega, Haruni M'Bega, Musa Funga, Nuhu of Mamboya
Front row: Yohana Malacela, Joshua of Berega, Andreya Lungwa, Reubeni Chidahe, Luka of Berega, Andereya Mwaka, Eliezer Balisidiya
Courtesy CMS

stands in Kongwa, known as the 'gorofa'. Whilst building, West-gate found time to hold classes for students.

The report on the work at Mvumi in 1913 shows that there were 1,000 less pupils than the year before; the enthusiasm of the first wave of interest had waned. There were still more people coming than the staff could adequately deal with, and the number of outschools had increased. In some out-stations a second had been opened as an offshoot of the first. Christian women had been conducting a women's school, and at outsta-tions teachers wives were having great influence. Attendances at the dispensary had numbered 4456 that year.

> Great as is the privilege of being permitted to see such mass movements, the strain which they involve ... can hardly be esti-mated. ... In this Mission there was also the disadvantage that no fully trained native workers were available, nor a single native clergyman to help in shepherding the rapidly increasing flock. Although all the missionary's duties multiplied many times over until he seemed to be burning the candle in the middle as well as at both ends, it was not that which weighed most upon him and strained him at times almost to breaking point, but rather the thought of the thousands who were not being gathered in, but who might be won for Christ.*

This revival was still going on when war broke out, and corre-spondence from the field ceased. The subsequent events could only be re-told years later when it was all over. What follows is taken from letters written after the war.

> [Doulton] On August 6th 1914 we were gathered together at Kongwa for a meeting. Our business was finished and we had said goodbye to Archdeacon and Mrs Rees, bound for home on furlough, when we were met by a messenger which brought the news that England had declared war on Germany. After confer-ring together we decided that Dr Westgate and Mr Briggs should proceed to Dodoma and enquire from the District Officer there as to our position.

> [Briggs] After travelling all night and all the next day these two men reached Dodoma, and the following morning were granted

an interview by the German in charge of Ugogo. Very friendly relations had always existed between this official and the Mission.. Their reception was marked by considerable formality. ... He could not allow them any longer to engage in missionary work in his district or to exercise any further influence over the native population of Ugogo. He requested the missionaries to return at once to their stations and live there quietly, avoiding moving about and he especially ordered a total cessation of all missionary effort by both the European and native staff.

When the missionaries working in Ugogo returned to their stations they found the akida (a native government official) had been round and publicly denounced the iniquity of the English. He told the Christians, and especially the teachers, to sever their connexion with the English Mission ... and to destroy at once their Bibles, hymn books, Prayer Books, and all other books printed in England. ... No books were destroyed and no one apostatized, even the newest of the converts coming out boldly on the side of Christianity. Even the ordinary natives were never more friendly than during this time; the veranda of the missionaries' houses were crowded with them at all hours of the day, the chief of some district or other constantly appearing to assure them of his sympathy and his regret that missionary work was stopped, and announcing the intention of both himself and his people to resume their 'reading' as soon as these troubles were over.

[Doulton] We on the Ugogo side chiefly occupied our time in translational work ... We were practically prisoners and expected to confine our walks to a very short distance from our homes. Mr Nauhaus of the Berlin Mission has been our friend all through this sad time, to the best of his opportunity and power.

[Briggs] On 8 January 1915 the CMS missionaries had the pleasure of welcoming ten women missionaries belonging to the UMCA. *[A high-church Anglican Society who were working on the coast; 4 went to Mvumi, 3 to Berega, 3 to Buigiri].*

In the beginning of January 1915 the German Government began to oppress the Christians associated with the Mission. The Government arrested two teachers from Handali. These two were removed from their homes by night, and their friends were left quite ignorant as to their whereabouts. It seems clear that the only reason for this was that they had been accustomed to meet together in the house of one of their number every night and morning for prayer.

In May 1915 the Government of German East Africa decided to intern all English subjects.

[Doulton] On 30th May 1915 we were taken to Kiboriani. There is no time to tell you of our journey which was a very hard one. We reached Kiboriani shortly before midnight and thus our imprisonment began at our own CMS Sanatorium. I must sum up our time there from May 31st 1915 to Feb 2nd 1916 in a sentence or two. It was very rough living to say the least of it. The German who was placed over us had not, as far as any one of us has been able to discover, one redeeming feature in his character. The prisoners, who were principally Missionaries, were compelled to work, the men had to make boot pegs, build huts etc and all the ladies were compelled to knit socks and sew pants for the German soldiers. The food was very bad indeed and it is no wonder that many suffered from internal complaints.

[Briggs] Soon after the removal of the missionaries German officials visited the various mission stations and commandeered whatever property or personal effects of the missionaries they considered would be of any use to them. They obtained by this means a considerable quantity of European stores, including a good supply of kerosene oil, while the original owners were in the internment camps deprived of all light at night. It does not take very long to enumerate the different viands supplied .. Native flour made from uwele, a very inferior kind of millet, and very tough meat formed the staple food. No vegetables, sugar or groceries were supplied, and of these the prisoners only had what they could provide for themselves. One of the missionaries [guess who!] obtained permission to send to his station for fresh vegetables from time to time and when they came this German official took a very large share of them. What remained was greatly valued by the prisoners.

The restaurant was an open grass shed, quite dry inside when there was no rain, as dew at least never came through it! It afforded sufficient accommodation for all if they sat close together, which, as the cold on the mountain-top was sometimes intense and the shed was open on one side to all weathers, was not a bad thing to do.

Each prisoner of war at Kiboriani was provided with the top or bottom of a double decker bed, made of rough poles with coarse rope stretched across, and two blankets. Such things as mattresses the Germans either forgot or did not consider necessary.

The head guard was a man quite unfitted to have charge of a camp and nothing appeared to please him more than when he had it in his power to humiliate one of the prisoners, as often as not a woman, in the presence of the native soldiers. A junior guard who was there for a time, named Herr Schenk, was very pleasant to everybody, and often went out of his way to do kind acts, and life at Kiboriani was much more bearable after he came.

Another very great cause for thankfulness was the regular Sunday services with the Holy Communion. In the frequently trying circumstances incidental to that sort of life, and the presence sometimes of actual danger, it was a great joy and strength to meet together round the Lord's Table and be reminded there of all that He suffered on our behalf .. and some of the petitions in the Litany gained a meaning quite new.

In February the prisoners had to make two long marches and a short railway journey under 'trying circumstances' to move to Buigiri.

[Briggs] The first sight of the mission station was not a pleasant one. There were no merry laughing crowds of African Christians to meet the travellers such as in happier times never failed to greet new arrivals. A thick fence of thorn surrounded the premises ... the cowed aspect of the few natives who dared to peep through their doors at the prisoners as they passed, gave a fair indication of the means by which that thorn fence had been made.

There began to be rumours of an English invasion.

[Briggs] At length all doubt was dispelled by an offical admission that Moshi had been evacuated. After this nothing more was heard until suddenly a report came that they had occupied

Kondoa Irangi. Buigiri was only some eighty miles from this place and directly in the line of march by which the British would come to get possession of the central railway. The prisoners had but little time to speculate as almost immediately an order came for the removal of the whole party to Tabora.

[Doulton] On April 22nd, the eve of Easter Sunday, we were given half an hours notice to leave, and allowed one box each. At Kikombo we were all packed into an iron shed with 42 natives and there we spent a very rough 22 hours. [They were threatened with loaded rifles.] We arrived at Tabora on 24th April ... there were a large number of other prisoners, about 140 including Dr Westgate who was brought to Tabora when the rest of us were arrested [and went to Kiboriani] ... the discipline was even more severe. We have heard the sad news that after we left Buigiri our station was looted and burnt and everything destroyed, so my dear wife [he too had remarried] and I have lost everything. We must take joyfully the spoiling of our goods but I find it hard to part with all our precious books. I think we had about 600 volumes all told.

[Briggs] As time went on and the invaders closed in on all sides, the guards became slack over many things. Even roll call was often poorly attended, though individual guards made frantic efforts to prevent slackness in discipline, and there was still the danger of being put into the cells for three days 'strenger arrest' which meant being in darkness all the time. One day a special roll call for women was held, and the commandant came and informed them that the Germans were greatly distressed at the thought of holding women as prisoners of war! They therefore proposed that these should be given their freedom ... About a month later the question was again raised; they proposed to send all the missionaries out of the camp. Not very long after, guns were heard in the distance, and it soon became evident that a battle was in progress. All night the guns were deafening, and for the greater part of the next day. In the afternoon the missionaries went a little way outside the town whence they could see the flashes of the guns, and they met the wounded soldiers streaming in from the battlefield. On 19 September 1916 the Belgian main army came up, and the German troops after being driven back on Tabora, evacuated the town the same night, and the next morning the invaders marched in and took possession. That day will never be forgotten by the little band of English exiles who mustered there in the streets of Tabora to welcome the brave Belgian army. Of course the latter had not expected to find any English prisoners there, and the native soldiers took them all for Germans, one of them remarking as he marched past, 'We are coming to kill you tonight; we take no prisoners.'

There comes a time in the life of a prisoner of war when he almost feels that it was worth while losing his freedom. It is that precious moment when he has just regained it; for only he who has tasted the bitterness of being led by others 'where he would not' can fully enter into the joy of being once more master of his own movements. This feeling, together with intense gratitude to Almighty God Who had brought them safely through all their trials and dangers now almost overwhelmed those who for so long had been prisoners of hope.

The CMS missionary group consisting of Deekes, King, Mr and Mrs Rees, Mr and Mrs Briggs, Mr and Mrs Doulton, Mrs Pickthall, Miss Ackerman, Miss Miller, Miss Mellows and Miss Forsythe left Tabora on 3 October 1916 and went with a caravan north to Mwanza. They then went by steamer across Lake Victoria to Kisumu, and by rail to Nairobi, arriving on 22 October. From Nairobi they went down to Mombasa and took a ship back 'home'.

Westgage had been kept apart from the other missionaries through this ordeal. The Germans suspected him, and to some extent Doulton, of teaching their African teachers to signal to the English, and Westgate in particular was brutally treated. There were times when he was close to being shot. On being released in Tabora he did not head for home and his waiting family, but first he joined a caravan travelling east, determined to go and visit the Christians in Kongwa and find out what had happened to them. He met with a hearty welcome.

The German army had preferred mission people to work as porters, and looked for teachers to do this job first. After teachers they looked for any men of the village but especially those wearing Christian dress. It was very hard work being a porter, so the fear of being caught for portering caused many people to

switch back to native dress, burn their books, and have the traditional holes in their ears. Several old people in Mvumi today give
this reason for their pierced ears.

Whilst John was recuperating in England he received a letter
from Andreya Lungwa, which told something of his story:

> The head teacher of Mvumi, [is] safe and well. This is the first I
> have heard of Andreya and we very much feared he was killed,
> especially as we knew the German Government about Easter
> 1916 were searching for him and had put a price upon his head.
> It seems that Mazengo, the chief of Mvumi, hid Andreya. Later
> on he was given the choice of producing him or being hanged
> himself, and so he (Mazengo) 'died' and his people were able to
> prove his death to the satisfaction of the Germans. His people
> gave out that a lion had killed him, and showed blood stained
> garments etc and also a grave in the forest. This was believed by
> the German official .. Of course it was all a hoax and got up by
> the Mvumi people to save Mazengo and Andreya. Both are alive
> and quite well today.

Andreya had been away from Mvumi to visit a dying relative
when the soldiers came to his house. So Andreya's wife and
family were kept as hostages, and locked in their house which
was to be burnt. However the firelighter didn't manage to set the
house alight and they survived. The families of all teachers were
in danger, and had to hide in the fields during the day and
shelter at home only at night.

Mika Muloli's family were kept hostage, and so Mika had to
come out of hiding. He was tied behind a horse and forced to
run all the way to Dodoma, 40 kms away. He fainted at one point
and so was dragged behind the horse. He was imprisoned and at
one point Mika was punched in the eye and was permanently
blinded in that eye. He later told that although he was permanently hungry and beaten for asking for water, his main fear was
that he would be hanged. He prayed that if he had done something wrong he would be hanged first, and if he had not done
something wrong he would be set free. He was finally tried by
three German judges who found no reason to hang him. He said
he wanted to fall at their feet, he was so happy.

[Briggs] Almost immediately after the removal of the prisoners of war from Buigiri to Tabora the Government sent their native soldiers to the different mission stations in the Ugogo portion of the Mission. Their instructions would appear to have been to collect evidence by every means in their power against the Mission. The first station visited was Buigiri where the internment camp had been. The severe floggings which took place here – the report of which reached other stations – helped to warn some of the teachers of what they might expect, and this gave them the opportunity to escape and hide themselves. All, however, were not so fortunate, or they considered it their duty to stay at their posts and bear whatever should come; and so, as station after station was visited some teachers were found at each place.

The method employed seems to have been for the soldiers to accuse the teacher of acts hostile to the Government and to demand a confession. A certain amount of rough handling accompanied this demand. When this failed to produce the desired effect, the teacher was stretched flat on the ground and held there by two men, while a soldier flogged him with a whip made of rhinoceros hide. After fifteen to twenty lashes had been given, a halt was called and the lad again questioned, and if the confession they were trying to extort was not made the flogging was resumed. In this way two teachers belonging to Handali received no less than 110 lashes each, until at length the soldiers decided that it was no use to beat them any longer. Upwards of thirty native Christians, nearly all of whom were teachers, were arrested. . . . They put the Christians all into chains, just as if they were slaves in the hands of the Arabs in the old slavery days, and conveyed them away to a native internment camp at Tabora, where for many weary months they were working under the lash, with brutal native soldiers over them day and night. On several occasions they were brought in chains into the European internment camp and given the work of sweeping up the compound. Their wretched condition caused additional anguish to the missionaries, who, of course, were quite unable to help them or to do anything to mitigate their hard lot.

When the Germans were preparing to evacuate Tabora, and with that end in view established food depots along the route, they used the teachers belonging to the CMS Mission, along with countless other natives, as porters, and they were all taken away chained together by the neck. It turned out therefore, that when Tabora was finally surrendered to the Belgians, and the prisoners of war, both African and European, were released, only about twelve of these teachers were among that happy number. These went with the missionaries as far as Mombasa, from which place they eventually reached their homes. Most of the other teachers, whom the Germans took away with them, escaped on the road and subsequently made their way to Ugogo.

Letters since received from the teachers themselves speak of their joy in being back again in their homes and their thankfulness to God for taking care of them and restoring them to their families. They tell of great numbers of people joining the inquirers classes, and the schools being crowded out and the opportunities for work greater than can be coped with.

On their release from prison the missionaries were met with one piece of very sad news. Their beloved Bishop and advocate, Bishop Peel, had died of typhoid at Mombasa on 15 April 1916. His knowledge of them and of the area, the people and the work was dedicated and thorough. There had been enormous growth in the scale of their work under his leadership and they would miss him immensely. His successor, the second Bishop of Mombasa, Bishop Heywood, had previously worked as a CMS missionary in India and was consecrated a whole two years later on 21 April 1918.

CHAPTER 5

Reconstruction in Tanganyika 1919–1928

The war in German East Africa had ended before fighting ceased in Europe, and so the future of the region lay in limbo for a number of years. It was only in 1920 that the League of Nations gave responsibility to Britain for administering what was now called Tanganyika Territory. As a Territory, rather than a Colony or a Protectorate, it was Britain's moral responsibility to manage the country for the good of the people, and at such a time as there were native people seen as being able to administer and lead the country it would be handed back to them.

Ralph Banks demonstrating a favoured means of transport – a donkey
Courtesy Banks family

These limbo years took their toll on the work of the mission, just as the war had. Reverend Ralph Banks had been a new young CMS recruit heading for Tanganyika when war had broken out. He stayed in Nairobi for the duration of the fighting but in 1917 he was able to make an exploratory journey around the region and see what the situation was like.

The war in Tanganyika had caused the people much suffering, many were displaced, some were killed, and all lived in fear. The people were not able to maintain their regular pattern of plant-

Andreya Lungwa
Courtesy CMS

ing and harvesting, and much of the food stock had been commandeered by the armies. These factors, together with poor rains meant that once again there was very bad hunger in the years following. In the year of 1918 a virulent form of influenza swept across Europe and was brought to East Africa, reaching Tanganyika. Many people were already weakened with hardships and hunger, and everywhere the influenza caused many more fatalities. Very sadly one of these was Andereya Lungwa who died at Mvumi on 2 January 1919 and is buried in the old graveyard near to the Briggs's infant son. John wrote of Andereya Lungwa in 1918 'He has done good work in the Mission as a catechist, and besides helping to translate the Bible into Chigogo, has now for some years been the head teacher at Mvumi and one of the pillars of the Church in Ugogo.' Doulton called him 'one of the very best men in the mission'.

Those who had been prisoners of war were run down and in need of a rest; they had been through a very traumatic time and their families had not known anything of their fate. The news from Banks indicated that the mission stations had suffered serious damage and loss so the missionaries recuperating on leave were also keen to raise money for rebuilding and re-equipping the mission. CMS gave them permission to take up funds for their work while in England, and they agreed a special appeal target of £5,000.

John had an interview with the CMS secretary for East Africa, Manley, on 1 May 1918 to discuss the possibility of the Briggs returning. Manley wrote:

> Mr Briggs said that during the end of their previous furlough Mrs Briggs was in a weak state of nerves and Dr Harford ultimately decided that her nervous state was such that she should

not be separated from Mr Briggs and that it was better that they should go out together. At the present time Mrs Briggs's health is tolerable but it is evident that separation would bring about a nervous breakdown.

Both John and Violet were registered for passages to Tanganyika but in fact they did not return until late in 1919. The Mvumi mission buildings had been looted by the Germans during the war, and all the furniture had been taken away. It was normal for missionaries to take bedsteads with them from England, but heavier furniture was usually obtained at the coast. The difficulty now was that with the shortage of resources after the war this was probably not possible, so it was necessary to take more from England.

The main 'station house' that John had built back in 1900 was in such a poor state of repair that he declared it unsafe and they moved into the Pan Anglican thankoffering school 'using the large hall as a living room and the classrooms as bedrooms. A small temporary church had been erected and in this services were held and also school.' John was granted £1,000 to rebuild the station, with the plan of building two new houses on the crest of the hill near the old house.

The temporary Mvumi Church, opened November 1919
Courtesy Banks family

However it wasn't only the buildings that needed John's attention. There was a very large district of people who had faced many trials and struggled on; and although many teachers had not deserted their flocks they needed encouragement and oversight. The church was still very young.

Miss Jackson had been on leave when war broke out and she returned at the beginning of January 1920 'with great joy'. In

November she wrote a descriptive Annual Letter giving a vivid picture of how she spent her time.

> I have been very glad to be able to devote myself entirely to work for women and girls. We made a new departure in starting a separate girl's day school, instead of carrying on the mixed school which has so far been the custom in our mission. It is held for a couple of hours five afternoons a week and we get an attendance varying between 50 and 200. The numbers are affected by the cultivating seasons, by epidemics of sickness, and just now many of the girls are being kept away by the cruel circumcision custom which is considered necessary for their physical wellbeing. .. We have six Christian teachers, three married and three unmarried. The younger of these, together with the more advanced girls, receive special instruction three mornings a week. At present the teaching is very elementary, reading and writing and a little arithmetic, singing and drill and games, basketmaking and sewing, and of course Scripture.
>
> I go out once a week with Abigeli the Bible woman, a true missionary whose face beams when she gets a woman to make the great decision. We set out as early as possible in the morning to escape the heat. During the cultivating season the kayas are usually shut up, and we look for the women in the gardens. At other times we get a good welcome from them at their homes. We sit outside, as it is too dark inside for our unaccustomed eyes to see anything, not to mention smoke and dirt and other disagreeables. They produce as many three legged stools as they can, the rest of the company often sit on pumpkins. When they are not familiar with our message we usually attract attention by teaching the children an action song. Everybody comes to watch, and before they know what they are doing they are listening to the Good News. Very often some 30 or 40 collect at one kaya. The flies keep us busy chasing them, the calves get a mad attack and threaten to upset us with their antics, a tiny lamb mistakes the visitor for its mother, one of the audience is interested in extracting a jigger from her companions foot with a thorn, but the Spirit of God works and we seldom go out without getting new inquirers, or winning some backslider to return, or some children to come to school.
>
> Once a week I go to one of the outschools that can be reached by a journey of two hours or less. There are at least 23 of these

schools near at hand. Four of them are carried on by teachers from the home station. The others are outstations with resident teachers ... Before the war most of these places had buildings for schools, but the majority of these have fallen to pieces and have not yet been replaced. School is mostly held against a kaya wall, or a baobab tree, one cannot say under a baobab tree; the greater part of the year they are leafless but their trunks are like great rocks, which afford solid shade from the sun except at midday. ... I hope that the periodical visits are an inspiration to the teachers and a means of attracting new inquirers for them to teach. Many of the women have never seen a European before, and want to run away when she approaches. Often there is quite a discussion as to whether the visitor is a man or a woman.

Soon after Miss Jackson returned, a new recruit arrived in Mvumi, Rev. W. D. Cole, who had to get started learning the language but with his help 'school' was divided for the first time into boys and girls. He took responsibility for teaching the boys in the old unsafe Mission House which was propped up for the purpose.

Miss Forsythe returned to Mvumi in April. At the end of the year she sent in her report:

It is with very mixed feelings that one starts to write an Annual Letter after an interval of seven years, and the first is naturally one of intense thankfulness and joy at being allowed, once more, to be God's witness in the place where so many happy years of service for him have been spent, and gratitude to him for all his loving care and protection during the years of enforced absence. ... [I] was greatly cheered with the hearty welcome of both my fellow missionaries and native friends. Many of the latter had grown out of recognition and it was indeed a great joy and encouragement to find several of those whom I had had the privilege of teaching, before the war, both boys and girls, now grown up and become teachers themselves. My work since coming back has been – as formerly – dispensary work, classes for women and children and various odd duties. The dispensary work is of course well known as being one of the most fruitful ways of gaining the confidence of the people, and gives numberless opportunities of personal talks with them.

The little house which I had for women patients [maternity cases] was in very bad repair and quite unfit for occupation, but Mr Briggs is having it seen to and I hope to have it fit for use again shortly, and in this way be able to help the women here far more effectually than is possible in their own villages (which are so dirty and unsanitary) and with far less expenditure of strength. Their native huts, having no windows, are absolutely dark and when going in from the brilliant sunshine, it is quite impossible to distinguish any object, so the first thing to be done is have a hole broken in the wall so that the patient may become visible. She is generally lying on an oxskin on the mudfloor and the only way in which she can be properly examined is by kneeling down in the dirt by her side. The insects are usually fairly numerous under these circumstances, and in the rainy season one can expect the added delight of having a stream or two of liquid manure from the cattle yard, flowing at one's feet. In spite of these drawbacks, the work is a very joyful one and the little medical knowledge one possesses is wonderfully used by God as a means of help and blessing to the poor people.

John reported:

Our first work of re-construction was to enlarge the small church as the numbers attending services increased so rapidly we were not able to find room for them. Then the Bishop had promised to return in February for confirmation, the first held here since 1913 and we had to set to work at once and look up the Christians, many of whom had become scattered during the war. This put us in touch at once with the whole Christian community and they responded splendidly, about 150 being prepared and presented to the Bishop for confirmation, and no less than 250 being present at Holy Communion at that time.

The work in the Outstations had suffered as much as anywhere. In many cases the teachers were living in borrowed houses, their own buildings having fallen down, and a great many of the Outstations had to be re-built. Then the number of teachers had fallen off considerably and the present staff was found quite inadequate for the reaching of all the people who wanted to be taught once they heard we had returned. For the first few weeks Chiefs with their followers were coming in from all the places where we had once had Outstations or schools, begging us to begin work there again and it became imperative to increase the staff of our native workers. Lack of money was the great difficulty and there was also the extreme difficulty of providing them with food as the famine was by no means over, the Mvumi harvest having been a scanty one. We managed to arrange for a considerable increase as the year went on and our native staff was increased from some fifty to between eighty and ninety. It is still however insufficient to reach all the places where the people are asking for teachers. With all this building up of the Spiritual Edifice, that of repairing and rebuilding the material fabric had to go hand in hand. A great deal of my time had to be taken up with building operations, the re-building of the Station going on all the time.

Only six months after returning to Mvumi, Violet Briggs died very suddenly on 24 May 1920. She had been in perfectly good health and set out with her husband on a short itinerating safari. Only one day after leaving Mvumi she complained of a sore throat which grew worse and so she was taken to Dodoma and treated by Dr Stones, a CMS doctor there. Her condition deteriorated and four days later she died of diptheria. Doulton wrote from Mvumi:

Poor Briggs brought the body in here the same day, Mrs Stones accompanying him as the Doctor was not able to leave his patients. [That night] I arrived by train from Tabora and was met by Dr Stones with the sad news which well nigh dazed me for the moment, as it was so sudden and so utterly unexpected. I travelled all night and got here about 7 am and was able to take the funeral service. There was a good gathering of Wagogo when we committed the remains of our dear fellow-worker to the grave, and there is great sorrow here especially amongst the women who mourn the loss of their beloved teacher. The loss to our Mission is great, especially of course at Mvumi and we shall sadly miss our dear bright Mrs Briggs but we sorrow not even as others who have no hope but look forward (as I told the people at the grave yesterday) to the day soon coming when we shall meet the dear one again in the presence of our glorious master. Dear Briggs is being wonderfully sustained in his great sorrow. We feel that we ought to get him away from here for a while so tomorrow

he and I are going to Dodoma ... and after some days we shall go
to Kiboriani and do some translational work until the time of our
next Committee meeting on June 21st.

The grave of Violet Briggs, which is in the old graveyard and
probably near that of her infant son, can no longer be identified.
Her loss was felt, not only by John, but by Miss Forsythe who had
travelled with her on their first journey out in 1903:

> As one who has worked with her for over 18 years in close fellow-
> ship and harmony the personal loss is indeed very great, but the
> loss to the work here especially amongst the women it is impossi-
> ble to estimate. Her bright happy manner and loving sympathy
> were always a help and inspiration and her influence amongst the
> native women here is sadly missed.

The state of the mission buildings went on unresolved for a bit
longer, with John away and hardly in the frame of mind, when
his wife had just died, to build himself a new house. In September the Committee agreed that instead of building anew he
should rebuild and enlarge the present Mission house. The
reason for this change of plan was 'the extraordinary price of
materials' which made it impossible to build at anything like the
original estimate. It seems, then, that the long old house that
stands to this day on the west of the Mvumi hill, with immensely
thick stone and mud walls, is the same house that Bishop Peel
marked out in April 1900, built by John in that same year and in
which John and Rose made their home. It seems that the house
suffered greatly during the First World War, so that it needed
really major renovation and rebuilding in 1920-21. This is
supported by the memory of Timoteyo Zoya in old age; Timoteyo remembered that his father Maruko sent him to sweep that
house during the War, while the missionaries were prisoners.

The following year, 1921, saw a sifting of those seeking the
Christian faith. There started to be a majority of women in all
areas of the work, and so there were many baptised unmarried
girls who had no prospect of a Christian husband and so
perhaps this was one reason why many lapsed. Miss Forsythe
wrote of this in her Annual Letter for 1921:

Still when one sees the depths from which they have been brought and the powers of evil with which they are surrounded, one can only wonder at the few who do fall away, and thank God for his keeping power, manifested in the many who walk worthy of Him.

Soon after the war Annie Barling, then aged 31 years, and Amy Gelding arrived from Australia with CMS and were stationed together at Buigiri, since they were thought to be excellent, and it would seem complementary, companions for one another. Annie Barling came from a farming family and on finishing her schooling had been doing 'home duties'. Her referees described her as undertaking work with thoroughness, brightness and resourcefulness, though not an organiser. She had a longing to do medical mission work in Africa and did some nurse training before leaving. In July 1920 she wrote from Buigiri:

I arrived here on May 11th 1919 having spent sixteen weeks on the journey from Sydney. Since then my time has been spent chiefly in language study. Unfortunately there have been some rather big breaks caused by sickness. In the first month after my arrival I had an attack of malarial fever and in November an

attack of enteric fever which hindered all work for over two months. Besides my language study I have helped in the work at the Dispensary three days a week ... I thank God for His great goodness in bringing me here to Africa and giving me this work to do.

Miss Annie Barling
Courtesy CMS Australia

John, now aged 53, proposed to Annie Barling, (aged 33) in May of 1921 and they married at Buigiri on 1 August; the first time that John did not have to make a safari of several months in order to marry. Marrying an Australian meant that on future home leave they would need to visit England and Australia, travelling by boat of course, and still be back within a year.

Miss Jackson became responsible for the boys school as well as the girls school when Rev. Cole was moved on to Mpwapwa. She could not even begin to do this on her own:

> The African teachers, 5 male and 6 female, have been very faithful to their work, and cannot fail to influence the characters of their scholars. At the girls school there has been an attendance of between 50 and 100 for five afternoons a week during the year. About 25 girls can read in the Cigogo New Testament, 8 of these are reading Swahili and an English primer. ... The attendance of the boys is not as good as we could wish, though it has improved lately, averaging 52 during the last month. Perhaps a greater proportion of boys are more advanced in their education than the girls are, but the girls are quickly catching up to them. We hope not only to draw future teachers from this source, but to provide Christian educated men, who can take leading places in their country's history, as it is opened to the outside world. The teachers meet two mornings a week, and are taught in preparation for the afternoon school .. We must learn to trust the African Christians more and more for the spread of the spiritual truths of our message, but there are very few yet who can do more than the most elementary part of the educational side of the work.
>
> There is the usual difficulty in training the girl teachers. They are no sooner a bit proficient when they get married. However they can still fulfill their home duties, together with a daily afternoon school, though it makes them very busy. They have to go a distance for both wood and water and the daily flour grinding and cooking take time. We have become accustomed to teachers managing their class, together with a baby of any age from 10 days old. In fact, many of the scholars have small babies tied on their backs, and we get plenty of practice in mother craft.

With Rev. Cole's departure, Miss Forsythe had to take on responsibility for the teachers in the outschools, and their ongoing in-service training. There were between 25 and 30 of them who came to Mvumi one day a week, for whom she prepared lessons and corrected exercises. This work was in addition to her many other roles. She ran the dispensary, which treated an average of 200 people per week that year, but she had the wonderful help of 'an earnest Christian woman' Secelela Nhizwa; do you remember her? Baptised by Price and one of the co-founders of Mvumi Mission. 'She is a very great help, as she can look after a good number of the cases such as ulcers, coughs etc.' Miss Forsythe was also on call day and night for maternity cases now that she had been able to restart her little maternity ward. The three best male teachers had been sent to Kongwa College for a years training and while they were away Miss Forsythe had to stand in for them, paying weekly visits to two outschools where she taught classes.

Secelela was a very valuable assistant to Miss Forsythe:

> She is especially good at illustration and often, when I am at a loss for something which will press home what I have been saying, she will come in with a most apt native proverb or illustration taken from their ordinary everyday life. eg one day when talking to a patient and trying to impress on him the need for repentance and decision in view of Christ's possible near return, she illustrated it most aptly by saying 'its just like this. Suppose you went to the Coast to barter and one and another of your friends gave you money to buy things for them, but you spent the money on your own pleasures, do you think you would like to face them when you come back?' to which he replied 'No I should be afraid'. 'Yes' she said 'You would, but what about Christ? We don't know the day He is coming and if He still finds you squandering the gifts He has given you and above all rejecting His salvation how do you think you will feel?' He saw the point at once.

The native church continued to develop and on 21 August 1921 Haruni Mbega and Andrea Mwaka, both from other districts, were ordained deacons by Bishop Heywood. They were the first native Tanganyikans to enter the ordained ministry of that part of the Anglican Church and a cause for much rejoicing. Had

Andreya Lungwa lived he may well have been amongst that number. Doulton wrote

> One of the men ordained, Andrea Mwaka, has been appointed to the Buigiri district and I am looking forward to happy fellowship in the Gospel with him ... I have known this man as a consistent Christian for about twenty-eight years. We are now to have a properly constituted church council, and the Christians seem to be realising more their responsibility in the matter of self support, so that, if the Lord tarry, we may look forward eventually (although some of us older men may not see it) to a Church financed and governed by the African Christians themselves.

The titles* given to these two men were not given by CMS, but by the local Church Councils who approved the ordinations, and local congregations funded them. CMS in London would quite like to have controlled the giving of titles, but Bishop Heywood strongly resisted this.

Bishop Heywood visited again in 1922 and his visit was reported in the Mombasa Diocesan Gazette:

> Three hours march next morning brought me to Mvumi soon after nine. Parties of Christians came out to meet me, some at least a mile. Rev and Mrs J H Briggs, Miss Forsythe and Miss Jackson welcomed me at the station, and it was a pleasure to see the Mission House completed, for on both my previous visits the missionaries were putting up with a good deal of inconvenience and lack of privacy in one of the school buildings. The Missionaries even now are learning fresh incidents of those troubled times from Africans who suffered much but as one of them puts it 'we never realised the Lord Jesus was so near us, till we passed through those days'.

This visit marked a further new stage in the development of the native leadership. The Bishop's report continued

> Thursday saw us climbing the hill to Kiboriani, where 7,000 feet above the sea is the Mission sanatorium, with simple accommo-

---

* fixed sphere of work and source of income as condition to ordination.

dation sufficient for the entire European staff of the mission to spend a few days together as one family, a wonderful opportunity for the growth of mutual knowledge, sympathy and co-operation. ... A whole week was fully occupied here with Committees and Conferences, one of the most important being the launching of the newly formed Native Church Council in these parts. The African members took a keen interest and share in the proceedings. The report of their financial contributions for the past year was most encouraging, and some of the subjects they themselves brought for discussion eg the best means of fighting against intemperance made one feel very thankful.

Although the native church was advancing there was also frustration and discouragement: the economic situation in Europe became harder and consequently there was less money to support the work of the CMS mission in Ugogo, even though it was growing and needed more investment. CMS reduced missionary allowances by 20%, and threatened a further 10% cut. Despite opportunities to open up in new areas, it was nearly impossible to sustain the existing work financially and so these opportunities had to be passed over.

John wrote his Annual Letter for the year 1922:

> The 1922 harvest in Ugogo was a bountiful one and, as happened so often in the history of the Children of Israel, this increase in material blessings did not bring with it any perceptibly greater desire on the part of the Wagogo for spiritual things. More native beer was brewed than had been possible for years, and a corresponding increase of drunkenness was noticeable even amongst the christians, and many old heathen customs were revived. Attendances at Church, Schools and Classes fell off ... Several of our Christian men, having first given way to drink with consequent laxity in other directions, ended by taking heathen women as second wives, and fathers married their sons, or daughters, to heathen from whom they could get large dowries. The Elders of the Church did all they could to prevent this but in many cases were unable.

John lamented this state of affairs, but he was also sympathetic to the human problem:

Temperance work in some form or other has become a necessity but the very great difficulty in pushing it amongst our christians is the lack of any non-intoxicating native drink. If an ordinary native becomes a teetotaler his only drink here in Ugogo is very dirty tepid water, often decidedly brackish into the bargain; it is therefore not surprising when a christian man hot and tired and perhaps very thirsty, hearing that a big beer drinking is going on at a village near by and knowing that, with the customary native generosity and hospitality in these matters, he has only to go and ask to be supplied with as much of it as he can drink quenches his thirst with this stuff which in the end alas! so frequently drags him down again to the level of heathenism which by God's help he had once renounced. We are trying to persuade our Christians to adopt tea as a drink as a counter attraction to beer drinking but the wagogo are a conservative folk and they haven't yet acquired the taste for it in any marked degree. Also sugar just now is dear on account of the very high duty and this with the cost of the tea, which also carries a very heavy duty, makes beer as a drink much more readily obtainable than tea.

There was a considerable amount of sickness that year, since better rains go together with more mosquitoes. In the same Annual Letter John wrote:

There were a good many deaths amongst our native christian community, principally from malignant malaria of a cerebral type. In several cases it was markedly noticeable how differently the christians look upon death from the heathen. One young girl of christian parents gave a bright testimony to God's presence with her up to the end, and she herself led the family in prayer only just before she died.

Miss Forsythe was always a passionate advocate for the importance and value of medical care. She wrote about her dispensary work:

Judging by the number who come daily for treatment, seems to be much appreciated by the people. The numbers attending vary considerably, ranging from about 30 (only very occasionally do we get less than this) to 60 or 70, and the ailments from which they suffer are almost as varied; from a simple cut or attack of indigestion – which is always described as a snake inside – to some case requiring most skilful treatment, over which one feels absolutely hopeless, but which so often would yield readily to the knowledge and skill of a qualified Dr, and oh, how we long and pray for such an one to help these poor creatures in their dire need and suffering.

I should like to tell of one case which I think cannot fail to shew the very great need there is for a Doctor here. Some months ago I was at an outschool about 3 miles away from here and saw a young married woman only 16 or 17 years of age. She was sitting on the ground in the cattle yard in the midst of indescribable filth and seemed to be suffering greatly from a very badly poisoned foot. All the instep seemed to be one sore but as it was covered with some filthy native medicine I could not see the extent of the trouble. I told her uncle – who is the headman of the village – to bring her to the dispensary here and he promised to do so, but delayed for a fortnight longer and by then the trouble had increased considerably.

The evening she arrived I went to the [nearby] village where she was staying, to dress the foot, and oh the awful condition it was in and the thought of the agony the poor thing must have been suffering because of it made one's heart ache: the whole instep was one mass of corruption and the stench from it so awful that I could not bear it in the house but had to have her brought outside and even then it was only with the greatest effort I could stand it. I did what I could, and went down again next day to dress it and again had to have her brought out of doors. That night a baby was born to the poor creature, which complicated matters and made it impossible to have her taken outside for dressing, so I had to do the best I could in the dirt and dark inside.

I went day by day to look after her, giving her food as well as medicine, as her husband's people refused to help her, and according to native custom they are supposed to do everything for her at such a time. She seemed at times to be slightly better, but did not improve as I had hoped and prayed she would, and when she was able to be brought out of doors again I soon found out the reason. In spite of being dressed daily and kept as clean as possible maggots had begun to breed in the poor creatures foot and when it was put into a bath of strong disinfectant between 30

and 40 came out of it; this happened twice and I quite hoped it
would get better, but the trouble was far too deep seated to cure,
except by amputation, the flesh literally rotted off her foot, and
after I had been treating her for nearly a month found her disease
far beyond my power to heal. I tried to persuade her relatives to
take her to the Government hospital at Dodoma but they
absolutely refused and there was nothing to be done but send her
home, where she died in a few days. This is just one instance of
the result of treatment by a native doctor, it might be multiplied
many times and yet we are so often and so glibly told that 'the
heathen are best left to themselves, their own ways suit them etc'.
I am sorry to have to enter into such unpleasant details but
without it could not give a proper account of the case and I think
too that friends at home do not perhaps sufficiently realise the
awful sufferings caused by heathenism and witchcraft and the
need to combat them by every means in our power.

Miss Jackson had also been busy and her Annual Letter gives an
insight into her visits:

Another year of more or less plodding routine work for the
women and children of Mvumi ... We make regular visits to the
nearer villages. The Christian women take turns in accompanying me. ... Some of the women who seldom see a European do
not expect to be able to understand me. If my Mugogo companion says exactly the same thing that I have said they will listen,
and be impressed. The general idea before they are enlightened
by the Spirit of God, is that we want them to be our dependants,
and to leave all their customs for our foreign ones. They are
mostly very willing to say they will come to Church, or send the
children to school, whether they mean to do it or not. ... Sometimes they are busy cooking salt, or a dozen big pots of beer are
being tended, as they boil over a fire made in a trench dug in the
ground.

In 1923 a village east of Mvumi, Handali, and the area to the
south of it were formed into a new mission station with the Rev.
Cole returning to take up residence there and being responsible
for the work. At the same time the teachers who had been in
training at Kongwa returned and they were placed in out-

stations, away from Mvumi in place of some of the relatively untrained teachers who had been working there. These untrained teachers could then in turn receive further training, and in this way the work of the Church was strengthened.

If the ladies were so busy, what were John and Annie doing? John made a long journey around the outskirts of the district to the south, visiting the outstations that were rarely reached because of the distance involved. Notice what he did! 'During that time I re-organised the work in several of our out-stations, rebuilt and repaired the teachers houses and churches which in many cases were falling down, and encouraged the teachers to continue their efforts.' On return from this journey he and Annie went to Kiboriani for their annual holiday, 'Spending some seven weeks there and using the time to put the Kiboriani buildings in a thorough state of repair, and especially providing accommodation for our servants and the native delegates to the Central Church Council Meetings at Annual Conference time.' His holiday was spent doing what he loved, building and providing. In this case it was to provide accommodation for the native church leaders so that when the Bishop came they could be included more comfortably.

John was responsible for managing the money and was meticulous in his record keeping and orderly accounts. The reduced allowances meant that he could not afford to do some work that needed doing; when he travelled as a European he needed several porters to carry his camping equipment, and the porters needed to be paid for their labour. To save money he sent one of the senior Agents, presumably one of those men who had trained at Kongwa, on several journeys around the out-stations. He wrote of this:

> To give help and advice to the teachers and Christians, as it was so much cheaper to send him in this way than to itinerate round there myself ... In this way the teachers were encouraged and helped in their difficulties, and perhaps these visits will bear good fruit in the future by inspiring the Native Church to rely more on its own members and not so much on the European.

John wanted to hasten the day when the native people of the area could lead themselves in their own church life.

Another important role that both John and Ernest Doulton continued to have was as translators; they had now been speaking Cigogo and Swahili for more than 30 years.

> During the year a considerable amount of much needed translational work was done. Mr Doulton and I together revised and very considerably enlarged the Cigogo Hymn Book, a new edition of which has since been printed by SPCK and is now in use. Other translational work done during the year included Native Church Organisation Regulations and also lessons for Inquirers etc.

The Regulations might sound rather formal and officious but as any organisation grows and more work is delegated there is a necessary formalising that takes place. What had up to then been carried around in the missionaries' heads as an orderly way of doing things had to be written down. As more pastoral responsibility fell to the senior native church leaders they then had some guidance and were less likely to get into problems.

John and Annie wrote in their Annual Letter for 1923 of how they returned from their working holiday in September:

> And found practically the entire community living on the Mission, as well as the people round about, under the influence of drink. They had all brewed quantities of native beer, and the next day (Sunday) a large congregation gathered in church which was decidedly 'drink sodden'. The drinking bout lasted a whole week and when it was over we got to work. First of all we had special meetings for our native agents and tried to show them that they must be entirely free from this curse in order that they might help their companions to give it up. After a great deal of teaching and prayer, in which we had valuable help from our Bishop during his visit towards the end of the month, practically all our native agents signed a declaration that they would cease from brewing native beer or bringing drink into their house.

Miss Jackson continues the story in her Annual Letter for that year:

A pledge was drawn up with two clauses 1- that they would have no beer made in their houses 2- that they would try to give it up altogether. They were all ready to sign the first agreement, but of the six men teachers on the station, only two who felt their special need would sign the second. One of them is a member of a family of drunkards, and his Christianity has kept him sober for months at a time. Lately he and a number of workmen were away from home for a couple of months, doing repairs on the sanatorium. The day they came back, the women had a very large quantity of beer ready for them, according to Cigogo custom, and he, together with many others, was incapacitated for three or four days. And the saddest part to me was that his wife, who is one of my most trusted helpers, had made the beer that did the mischief. But at the meeting he stood up and said 'you know all about me, what I have been, long ago and these days. Now, in the name of Christ, I give up drink altogether.' The other lad, who made a similar pledge, said he was doing it because he found his mental powers were being destroyed. ... Since ... I have had a letter from him saying that his relatives have become his enemies because he is doing a thing which his ancestors never did. It seems to us that those who are still hesitating about promising never to drink beer – and the only alternative is muddy water – are being tested as to whether they are ready to give up all for Christ. We believe that, in answer to our prayer, they will come to full surrender, and will know the joy of being wholly His.

John saw the process as

A great step forward, especially as it is not easy to find an alternate drink (except water) which it is within their means to procure. We have tried to help them with tea and sugar and a good few are drinking this now, but some who have only a very small wage have a difficulty in finding the money to pay for it even though we supply them at less than cost price. I am glad to say that since the meetings ... a very great improvement has taken place amongst the general christian community, and some well known drunkards have come forward of their own accord and pledged themselves to give up drink.

The Bishop's annual tour ended in October 1923 on the hilltop at Kiboriani, for the general Conference of all missionaries and for the new Church Council meetings. He wrote of this in the Mombasa Diocesan Gazette:

> On three of the days delegates from all the African centres joined with us. There is no doubt that they are beginning to realise what an opportunity these African Church Council Meetings give them, and we hope and pray they will use them more and more.

Kiboriani

I am writing from the Sanatorium of the Tanganyika Mission, where the majority of the CMS missionaries are staying on after Conference for their annual holiday. We are getting rest and refreshment to body and spirit in this place of 'far stretching lands and mighty mountains', and also in communion with our fellow-workers. We are having daily gatherings for Bible reading and prayer, especially for revival, in ourselves, and in our African fellow-workers. The annual visit of our Bishop has been an inspiration to us all.   Effie Jackson 1923

Miss Forsythe, in a letter written at the end of 1923, made a heartfelt cry for the dispensary work which was:

> Decidedly more difficult and the people less responsive than before the war and this I think can be accounted for by the fact that during the years when they were without help of any kind, many of them reverted to their old custom of going to the native witch doctors for treatment and the power of these men has consequently much increased. Just lately we have had evidence of this in the death of two or our leading Christians. In both cases the sick people wanted us to attend them and their heathen relatives humoured them so far as to come to us for medicine, but later on we found in both cases that the medicines had not been given, neither had our instructions been carried out and unfortunately we did not discover this until it was too late to save their lives. Oh, I wonder <u>when</u> are the home Committee going to (may I say with all reverence) help God to answer our prayers of years by sending us a Doctor to help these poor people in their sore

need. ... I write as one who has had 20 years experience of life and work amongst the people and so can claim some knowledge of their characters, needs etc.

The year of 1924 saw the resources of the mission stretched even more. Mr and Mrs Deekes, who had been amongst the pioneering missionaries and been John's companions on his first voyage out, had retired the previous year after 36 years service. Archdeacon Rees, who had married John and Rose in 1900 and had been in charge of the theological education at Kongwa after the war, died in Dar es Salaam on 24 March 1924 after 27 years of missionary service in Tanganyika. John and Annie were due leave at the beginning of April and they left for the coast with the widowed Mrs Rees, she to return to Britain, and they to go to Australia. Andrea Mwaka and Haruni Mbega were ordained to the priesthood on Ash Wednesday and they, together with the remaining missionary priests, made a total of only six ordained men to minister to the Christians of Ugogo and Ukaguru – a vast area.

The work undertaken was nevertheless considerable. Miss Jackson only found the time to make her report when she was on holiday at Kiboriani Sanatorium. She wrote

I have not statistics for the year here but the average attendance for July and August was – Boys 35, Girls 60. There was a much larger attendance of both boys and girls during September and October, and we hope the boys especially will not quickly tire again, but will take advantage of the privileges provided for them. They are beginning to get interested in their handwork. When it was introduced they despised it, and stayed away the day it was on the timetable, saying there was no school that day. But now they are learning to make mats from reeds, which will be useful to spread on the rope nets of the wooden bedsteads, which are gradually being introduced instead of skins spread on the ground. They have already learnt to make rope and brooms from the baobab bark, and are also learning to carve wooden spoons, to the accompaniment of cut fingers. ... The majority of the scholars are learning to read and write, with arithmetic, drill, and singing to vary the programme, but a proportion are learning

African History and Geography, Hygiene, Swahili and English. Every afternoon we have the Scripture lesson, and try to fulfil the primary reason of our schools existence, that of winning souls to surrender to Christ, as the rest of the training should be helping them to live for Him. The babies, who come tied on the backs of their little sisters, have a heap of sand in which they delight to play, and quickly get accustomed to the strange looking European, who strikes terror into their hearts when they first see her.

There are 6 male and 5 female teachers on the station and 53 male teachers living at 25 out-stations. From these outstations they work one or two weekly schools so that the number of centres reached is 68. The total scholars for the district ... are 2572, (1461 male and 1111 female). ... We praise God for what it has been possible to do, for men and women living new lives, and for boys and girls who have learnt, or are learning, high Christian ideals.

However the issue of drunkenness recurred, this time at the time of the boys' initiation ceremonies.

All the moonlight night there was the sound of revelry, one of my women helpers was beaten and driven from home by her husband and next day we heard of one after another of our trusted folk who had fallen. One was tempted to despair, but there was much penitence expressed at our next prayer meeting, and there have not been such bad falls since. Still one feels we must put on the whole armour of God to fight against this evil, as well as others, with which the great Enemy tempts these inexperienced Christians and causes the name of Christ to be blasphemed among the heathen.

While John and Annie were away Miss Forsythe found it very hard to manage their work.

Soon after Mr Briggs left we sent our right hand man here – Mika Muloli – to visit the further off outstations and report on the work carried on. He is a most earnest, devoted follower of Christ and absolutely trust worthy and his account of the work was not very encouraging. Several of the teachers had grown cold, and others were actually doing no work whatsoever, and yet receiving their wages regularly. The result of his itineration has been the dismissal of the most unsatisfactory ones and we have had a good deal of difficulty in finding others to take their places.

Miss Forsythe was understanding though, of the difficulties these teachers faced. She continued:

> Think of the numbers of conventions, missions, etc which are thought necessary at home and these – in addition to the usual Sunday services, Bible classes and all the other numerous helps they have. Then try and picture what it would mean to have one, or at the most two, very ignorant inexperienced Christians put right away in the midst of people who are not only unsympathetic, but antagonistic often. With no outside helps such as meetings, classes, ... fellowship etc not even church services except those which they themselves conduct and with nothing but heathenism and wickedness all around. I think the love of many even earnest, devoted Christians would grow cold under such circumstances and God's work suffer as it has suffered here. We need greatly at least two keen, energetic young men who could give their time to going round the district, supervising the work, and helping and strengthening the workers. Some of these in the far off places have not had a visit from a missionary since before the war.

There was much praise for Paulo Chidinda in Miss Forsythe's report; she told of the difficulties faced by the Christians in Handali, where he was the teacher:

The chief there has done all he can to hinder the work even going so far as to threaten to set fire to the houses of those who sent or allowed their children to go to school. The head teacher there, Paul Chidinda, has been his special target and has had to suffer much because of the lying accusations

Paulo Chidinda
Courtesy CMS

brought against him by this man. He had him tried at the Dodoma Court on absolutely false charges and succeeded in having him heavily fined, while 3 Christians, one a teacher, whom Paul had as witnesses, were imprisoned for a month each. Then in addition to all this trouble, Paul has had a very trying anxious time with his wife who has been seriously ill for months and is, I fear, incurable, but through all he has been so brave and his faith in God so real and deep that it has been a lesson to me and a rebuke more than once when talking to him. He has kept the work going and taught the people so well, by example as well as precept that the offerings from there for God's work are much more than those of even our Christian congregation here at Mvumi, and this in spite of the fact that for the past 3 years the harvests at Handali have been very bad indeed. ... A much greater proof tho' of his zeal and God's blessing on it is that in the midst of all his trouble and anxiety, several adults from there came forward and confessed Christ in baptism after having been carefully taught and prepared by him. Seeing such a wonderful illustration of God's great power manifested in such a way in one of these heathen people is a great encouragement.

The lack of support from CMS for the work in Tanganyika was still as much a struggle as ever. Miss Forsythe finishes her letter with a plea. 'I should like in closing to once more try and press home the very great need we are in for more workers.'

John and Annie returned to Mvumi at the beginning of April 1925 and were present at the Conference held at Kiboriani at Easter. John's old friend Ernest Doulton at Buigiri had been acting as Secretary of the Mission for some years; a job which involved having day to day responsibility under the Bishop and CMS for the work in Tanganyika, for the care of staff and management of money. John took over this position as soon as he returned, since Doulton was forced to retire through ill health after an eventful and productive 31 years on the field.

John Briggs had come a long way from the junior nurseryman who had first set off for East Africa; now, at the age of 57 he was moving beyond the role of chief in Mvumi and taking on the role of elder statesman in the region. His extensive knowledge of the area, of the languages and the peoples, and his care for them, together with his excellent practical skills, his faultless administration and account keeping, meant that he was able to contribute significantly in almost every area of the church's work there.

With the retirement of Mr and Mrs Doulton from Buigiri the number of staff covering this large area of central Tanzania was at its lowest level. However the British Government's administration of Tanganyika had had time to find its feet and see where it was going. In 1925 missionaries from all over the country were invited to a conference with the highest Government officials to discuss and find a common policy for Education. John reported the event as follows:

> The Education Conference in Dar-es-Salaam last October, which was attended by three members of the CMS staff in this Mission, was a wonderful gathering. When His Excellency, Sir Donald Cameron, the Governor of this Territory, at the opening of the Conference publicly announced his acceptance of the Memorandum of the Advisory Committee in Downing Street, as the 'Charter of Education for Tanganyika Territory' the utmost hopefulness and enthusiasm pervaded the whole assembly, and as day by day went by and problems were straightened out, mainly through the great sympathy for, and understanding of, the evangelistic side of missionary work, shown by the able Chairman of the Conference, Mr Rivers-Smith, the Director of Education, and his evident wish that in the educational work done by the Missions, religion should not be left out, this feeling deepened and increased, until at the close both Government Officials and Missionaries felt that it had been 'good to be there', and the Chairman requested one of the three Bishops who were present to gather up as it were the feelings of all in a comprehensive Offering of Thanksgiving to Almighty God for what He had enabled us to accomplish.

This remarkable meeting resulted in the promise of Government grants to Missions for their educational work. The Government would pay the salaries of any missionaries who were 'educationalists' ie who had teaching qualifications, and who would be teaching in a Mission school in Tanganyika. The Government would set the syllabus, and the schools would be liable to inspection. Miss Taylor at Buigiri and Rev. Cole at Handali qualified immediately but no other CMS missionaries had suitable qualifications.

John continued:

> It now remains for the Home Committee to enable the CMS in Tanganyika Territory to take advantage of the splendid openings there are, if only the staff required can be sent out quickly. £11,000 have been budgeted for by the Education Department of the Territory for 1926, as Grants-in-Aid to Missions, and CMS can claim a share of this if they will send out Educationalists with the teaching qualifications required by Government.

The work of educating people so that they could provide their own leaders and teachers was more important then ever as the church grew in number and maturity. 'All day school' started for the first time in Mvumi in this year and the pupils were showing good results but with the constant strain of work it was difficult to make more progress in the area of education. Kongwa training college had been closed ever since Rees died and so John continued training the teachers by bringing them to Mvumi for two days each month for in-service training. It is remembered by the children of these teachers that they collected their pay at the same time – a good way to make sure all attended. The educational grants must have been a great encouragement, CMS had been close to withdrawing from Tanganyika, but when they received news of the grants they took it as Gods challenge to them to send more people instead.

In July 1926 Bishop Heywood received a cable from the Australian branch of CMS which said the following: 'propose to give increased financial support and extra workers when available and assume greater responsibility for Tanganyika Mission aiming at raising additional £2000 within 12 months'. It had even been suggested in Australia that Tanganyika be taken on as their own special Mission, and this was indeed what was to happen. Australia had long had an involvement in the work, both Miss Jackson and Annie Briggs were Australians, but now instead of supporting the work of CMS through the office in Britain they would be primarily responsible. The missionaries' response to this suggestion was one of welcome, since they hoped that it would mean the work would be able to develop again after a long period of being under-resourced. At the same meeting the Bishop told of his suggestion to CMS that the Diocese of Mombasa should now be divided – the work had grown too great.

The new education policy meant the opening, towards the end of 1926, of a Girls Boarding School at Buigiri by Miss Taylor, and a Boys Boarding School at Handali by Rev Cole. Some of the more advanced Mvumi scholars were sent to these schools. John's report for the year described the £1000 grant from the Director of Education to CMS as 'epoch making'. 'We hope that such Grants will now be a permanent annual assistance to the educational work of the Mission, and that the grant for 1927 will be doubled as compared with that for the year under review.' There really were signs of hope that, after all the years of struggle to improve the education and leadership of the native people, the opportunities would be provided at last.

However Education wasn't the only area in which the Government were making bold initiatives as John also recorded.

The Government has published a Native Authority Ordinance which gives very wide administrative powers to the Native Chiefs. In fact it aims at restoring to them to a very great extent the authority which they possessed over their people before the advent of the European Governments in East Africa. This has resulted in a great number of cases in acute attacks of 'swelled head' on the part of the chiefs and their headmen, and they have interpreted this restoration of their power to mean that heathenism is to be encouraged because it was the old order of things.

Under this Ordinance the Government are now ruling indirectly through the chiefs and tribal councils instead of issuing orders directly as they formerly did. This means that the chiefs are expected to take the initiative much more than they were ever allowed to do under the former regime, and the lack of constant reminders of things they are expected to do, by their District Officers, makes them regard the Government as becoming slack, and results in indifference on their part in regard to the education of their people and other means of progress. A lack of restraint on the part of the people was manifested, especially in beer drinking and other forms of indulgence, which has had an influence on our Christians and Mission Adherents, resulting in smaller attendances at Church, fewer baptisms, and less desire for religious instruction with a view to baptism. Of course this is inevitable at the beginning of a new era, and the Native Authority Ordinance is a real sign of progress, for which we thank God, and will without doubt have a beneficial effect in course of time on all our Native Church Organisations, by teaching the people to govern themselves.

Miss Forsythe had been on leave and came back in mid-April with something fun.

I am thankful to say that the women have been coming much better since I got back and have been able to start regular teaching again. A gramophone which I brought back with me, the gift of friends in Ireland, has been a great attraction to them and has, undoubtedly, been the means of bringing some who would not have come otherwise, and great is the disappointment if, for any reason, they cannot have a short musical programme at the end of the Scripture lesson.

The Australian church invited Bishop Heywood to visit and early in 1927 he went to enlist the sympathy and support of the Church there for the proposed new diocese. As a result of this visit, the Australian Church Missionary Society accepted that responsibility. It was therefore appropriate that the Archbishop of Canterbury should look to Australia to supply its first bishop, naturally strengthening the links between the diocese and CMS Australia. So it was that George Chambers was invited to England and on 1 November 1927 the Diocese of Central Tanganyika was formed with his consecration, at Canterbury, as its first bishop. Bishop Chambers was 50 years old; he was a man of confidence and enthusiasm who was able to inspire others to offer themselves for service, or to give money for the Diocese, (he launched the Diocesan Association the next day). One of his recruits (Avis Richardson) wrote later in her memoirs:

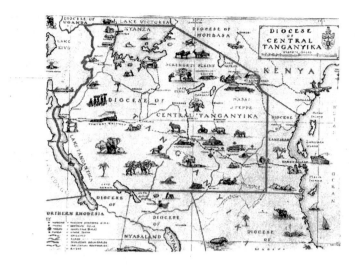

Map of the new Diocese of Central Tanganyika – still a vast area
Courtesy Banks family

He showed right from the beginning of his appointment that he would be a truly dynamic bishop and the appeals he made for people to trust the Lord, to give to the new work and to offer for service in the new diocese, aroused tremendous interest and a great response. His own anticipations were great. ... Enthusiasm was certainly aroused in his hearers whenever he spoke.

There were significant changes for John too – the Mission was given the gift of a motor car, and this was allocated to him as Secretary since his work involved him in considerable travel. Imagine what excitement this car must have caused in Mvumi, and what new games for the children to play. (Spectacles had already influenced facial paint designs for dances) A different era indeed from 1892 when John made his first caravan journey up from the coast.

Mazengo 'the enlightened and progressive chief of Mvumi' was made President of the Tribal Council for the South of Ugogo in 1927. He announced that he wanted all the children to be taught, and his influence brought more children to the mission school than would otherwise have gone. That year there were 7 boys from outlying dis-

Chief Mazengo and Mika Muloli
with a young Filemon Chidosa on
the far left

tricts living with friends in
Mvumi so that they could attend
Miss Jackson's day school; of
these 2 were the sons of Chiefs.
At Christmas time that year
Chief Mazengo came and pre-
sented the school prizes. Miss
Jackson described it.

Each child who had attended a
good percentage of days was
called by name and came up
and received, politely with
both hands, a garment from
the hands of his Chief. Others
received prizes which were
donated by the Director of
Education for writing and mat
making. And last of all the tiny
ones each received a garment. Some of them had to be piloted
up to the Chief as he sat in his chair, and presented in regal
fashion. Others who had not been provided for brought themselves along expectantly. Each prize winner was applauded and
one boy marched up vigorously applauding himself! Finally the
Chief made a short speech encouraging the children to attend
school regularly.

The lessons had included some agriculture.

Twice a week we go early to the garden, which should introduce
them to a new diet, and improve their stamina, besides showing
them that education is not only reading and writing. We have
planted cassava and sweet potatoes, which the Wagogo do not
cultivate extensively, and bananas and pineapples, mangoes and
pawpaw, and tomatoes, all of which need constant watering in
the dry season, and a few years ago were unknown here. We are
even trying a competition between the classes as to who can get
the best watermelons in the dry season. The tomatoes have done
very well, and about 70 have been distributed three times a week
for some time.

The smallest children coming to the day school were given bananas or a drink of milk whenever it was available, no doubt supplied from John's garden and cattle herd.

A letter to Miss Jackson from one of the out-station teachers gives a graphic account of native witchcraft. (The chief mentioned is not the Chief of Mvumi.)

> I want to tell you what my wife and I saw of the lost condition of our people here. The Chief called all the head men of his district, perhaps there were 50 of them, and they brought about 30 stools and about 200 stones, and 3 sheep. And they drew a lot of water as if they were going to make mortar for building, and they bathed the stones on the stools. When they had finished that, they took one of the sheep and killed it, and melted the fat (of the tail) and rubbed the stones with it. Then they took the other two sheep and some holding the front legs apart, others on each side, pierced them with knives. Alive as they were, when the blood flowed, they held out the stools with the stones arranged on them so that the blood dropped on the stones. That is what the head men did who were called, they said to the spirits of the people who had died, So and So, let the rain come, and they want female rain, not male. (Female rain means steady showers, male rain means wild thunder storms.) They say they clean the rain. Well, that is what we saw yesterday here at our place.

Miss Forsythe's work continued as ever. 'The dispensary attendances from Jan to August number 4412. A large number of whom were fever cases, with a fair percentage of ulcers and sores of various kinds.' The 3 bed maternity ward was showing a benefit, since after the women delivered she was able to teach them about infant welfare and hygiene.

> 'The infant mortality is appalling and it is quite the ordinary state of affairs for women to have only 2 or 3 children living out of a family of 12 or more. In this respect one sees a very marked difference in the families of those women who have benefited by this help and teaching and instead of the 2 or 3 one sees families of 7 or 8 strong healthy intelligent children whose bright happy faces are a real encouragement, and make one feel that the seed sown in what so often seemed to be such hard stony ground, has

indeed taken root and we look forward with hope and confidence knowing that He who has worked in the past will not fail to do still greater things in the future if we are faithful and believing.

1928 was a watershed in many ways, as the old slipped away and the new stepped confidently in. The Government published a new Ordinance prohibiting the use of porters for carrying loads in areas where motor transport could be used, presumably because it was associated with slavery. John wrote to his new bishop about the costly implications of this. 'When this comes into force we may have to hire Indian lorries to convey our goods to our station, which will be much more expensive than having our own motor lorries.'

In April the Committee met as usual to discuss matters of concern; staffing, funding, planning, and this included the question of the Buigiri girls school which was going very well with 60 girls in residence, but was still in temporary mud buildings. They made a report:

> The Executive Committee, having carefully considered the question of the permanent location of the Girls Boarding School at present in temporary quarters at Buigiri unanimously came to the conclusion that, for many cogent reasons, it should be transferred to Mvumi and permanent buildings be erected there as soon as possible.

What were the cogent reasons? Firstly they thought that the water supply was better at Mvumi, an important factor for building as well as for the needs of a large school community. Another factor was that when missionary teachers were away on leave, it would be easier for other missionaries and teachers to cover their work if the school was at Mvumi. In addition, the Government was concerned for the training of African nurses. They asked the mission to include maternity training in the education of the girls, and to build the school next to a proposed hospital at Mvumi. The estimated cost of building what was to become Mvumi Girls Boarding School was published as £500 of which £135 had been raised. A missionary builder, Noel Forsgate, arrived at the end of 1928 to be responsible for this and a new period of expansion was underway for Mvumi.

This period of expansion, buildings and money to manage, as well as the staff and resources to use them, meant more work for John, the Secretary. The Committee pleaded for assistance for him and he was given the promise of his own secretary, 'Secretary's Clerk'; Miss Milsom was to set sail in the new year.

Bishop Chambers

After his consecration in England Bishop Chambers returned to Australia to raise more people and funds before arriving in Tanganyika. He was enthroned at Mvumi on 2 November 1928, for which a new church was specially built with thick stone walls and a flat native style mud roof. This 'new church' is now the 'old church of St Peters' renovated in 1997-8, and still in use as a place of worship. John supervised the building of this church, and to get wooden posts (nguzo) tall enough to have a suitably high roof, and rafters (miamba) long enough to make a decent span, he went as far as Mansase. A man called Sirikale Mhumba was in charge of choosing the posts and rafters; John gave him a piece of rope to measure each post and rafter, and nothing shorter would be accepted. The posts and rafters were necessarily of an extremely hard wood, and were therefore very heavy. They were carried to Mvumi, two or three men to each piece.

Narelle Bullard was one of the new party of missionaries from Australia and she described events in a letter to her family:

Mvumi looked wonderful, every house on the station was freshly cemented – a nice large church had just been completed, the village school was the dining room and the old church served as sleeping quarters .. Next morning was the native enthronement, the church was packed, we all sat in seats arranged each side on the chancel, the native men were one side, the women the other. The two native clergy took part in the procession as they stood waiting for Bishop Heywood to scrutinize the documents after the Bishop knocked for admittance. The service of course was in Cigogo but the Bishop preached in English and Mr Briggs interpreted. Then Mr Briggs was made Archdeacon of Dodoma in English by the Bishop and that was all interpreted into Cigogo again. Then followed Holy Communion, the Bishop administered. He said 'sole ulye' (take you eat) and when he forgot he put it backwards 'ulye sole' (you eat take). It was a very beautiful service and quite long. We did justice to the wonderful lunch prepared. Mrs Briggs organised that part of the conference wonderfully well, everything home made and 40 of us. Station life here is a little different from Kongwa, everyone is called to Church, school and meals by a native drum which is beaten first at 6am, it is a beautiful sound.

The new church was consecrated by the new Bishop just a few days later, when Bishop Chambers returned to Mvumi to spend a few days in conference with the missionaries (now numbering about 40). Mvumi had taken over from Kiboriani as the best place for such meetings since there were too many people for Kiboriani to accommodate; it had been outgrown. Annie was in charge of the catering and housekeeping, having the benefit of John's beautiful garden, and John was in charge of the administration and keeping everything in order.

It seemed that a new day was dawning for the Mission. John wrote

We have been very much cheered and encouraged by the prospect of the Australian Church coming to the help of this Mission and we look forward confidently to the coming years being so fruitful that they will make up for the past lean ones, and that in this way God may indeed restore to us 'the years that the locust hath eaten'.

CHAPTER 6

Bishop Chambers and the Diocese of Central Tanganyika 1929–1938

The core group of missionaries based at Mvumi had been stable for twenty years; John Briggs and one of the Mrs Briggs, Miss Jackson and Miss Forsythe. Now this began to change. Miss

Forsythe was called upon to work elsewhere in the Diocese; her experience and knowledge of the Cigogo language and customs was very valuable, and as the new wave of missionaries arrived and were posted around the Diocese they needed someone to teach them and mother them in their often lonely postings. In March 1929 she was requested to work at Kongwa, later she was at Mpwapwa, and then in the 1930's she worked in the far west of the Diocese at Rubongo. She retired in 1941, after 38 years of tireless service, most of which were at Mvumi. Because her last years were away from Mvumi she is

Miss Forsythe in retirement in
England about 1948
Courtesy Banks family

not remembered so clearly there, although many will tell you that they, or their parents, were born in Bibi Forsythe's clinic. She died in Cheadle Hulme, Cheshire, at the age of 81.

Narelle Bullard's letters

I love Tanganyika but I can't think it beats Australia – Miss
Forsythe says wait a bit, it isn't in your bones yet.

Noel Forsgate got to work on the biggest building project Mvumi
had yet seen, the Mvumi Girls Boarding School. The work
employed one hundred men, and the school was built on the east
side of the low Mvumi hill, from grey granite blocks cut carefully
from the nearby hillsides. There were eleven dormitories built
around three sides of a square, whilst a common room and
kitchen formed the fourth side. This was on the same plan as a
native house. These rooms surrounded a large paved courtyard,
with verandahs built along all the inside walls of the dormitories.
The bathrooms were in an inner courtyard leading from the first.
There was also a block of classrooms and a big hall, as well as
accommodation for two houseparents and their family, and a
European staff house with enclosed courtyard. Large deep water
tanks were dug out in each courtyard, lined with cement and
covered over with corrugated iron. Each one had a trapdoor
enabling water drawers with bucket and rope to draw out fresh
rainwater for drinking and cooking but strictly nothing else,
since rainwater was much sweeter than the rather salty ground-
water carried from the wells for washing and cleaning. By the
end of 1929 the building was still not finished and there was no
money left to carry on with. A temporary roof was added so that
the European teaching staff and the 70 girls from Buigiri could
be accommodated and school there began in the new year of
1930.

Rev. Ben Lousada was another new Australian recruit to
Mvumi, sent to strengthen the work that Miss Jackson was doing.
Miss Millsom had arrived to assist John and the Bishop with the
growing administrative burden of managing the work of the
Diocese, and Miss Thornton a trained nurse, arrived to take over
responsibility from Miss Forsythe for the dispensary work. At
some time before this a tennis court had been built just below the
long old station house, and tennis games played there are still

remembered by local people. Children who acted as a ball girl/boy were rewarded with a sweet at the end of the match for their trouble.

Annie's parents were both over 80 and so in early 1929, when John and Annie were due home leave they went first to Britain, then in August sailed to Australia to visit them. Now that the work of the diocese had much stronger links with Australia this meant that John could continue what he called the 'Tanganyika Campaign', begun so ably by Bishop Chambers. As Secretary of the mission and with 36 years experience he could speak with authority and knowledge. While John and Annie were away the Bishop had taken on the role of Acting Secretary, meaning that he was responsible for the day to day management. In this time the Diocese ran into serious financial problems as CMS in Britain wound down its support of 'All Other Heads', being the money sent to support native teachers, costs of travelling around to support native teachers, and also to cover the cost of dispensary work. CMS Australia had not yet taken these costs on, so the Diocese was caught in between. To add to the problem, CMS Australia was not sending on money that had been budgeted and approved for Tanganyika. Appeals were sent to both and economy measures taken to tide the gap.

Bishop Chambers was a gifted fundraiser and inspirational leader. However, as with everybody, he had his blind spots. Some notes written by Ralph Banks while John was away imply that there was a difference of opinion at times between the Bishop and Archdeacon Briggs. If it suited the Bishop better to reallocate money that had been given for a specific purpose, whether that be supporting a particular missionary or for a piece of building work, then it was not beyond him to do that. That created problems for those coming along behind keeping the records and being accountable to the home societies. Firstly it might make it difficult with those people who had given the money, and secondly those missionaries who thought that their work was provided for then found that the pot was empty!

The Bishop tended to make decisions about who was to be sent where, and which areas would become new mission stations, without consultation with those who would be responsible for carrying on the work. When the area had been part of the Diocese of Mombasa the Bishop was far removed much of the time and took the advice of those who were there and knew what should be considered. It must have been quite a shock to the system for John and the other senior missionaries to adapt to this new situation where they were trying to catch up all the time, and pick up the pieces of what Bishop Chambers had decided.

The Bishop could be quite lavish in his expenditure. On one occasion he wanted to go on a tour and he got his young protégé, Rev. Wynn Jones, to drive him. They had a breakdown so the Bishop borrowed another car and left the first car in the bush. They went on until the second car broke down. The owner complained of rough driving and so the Bishop had to buy the second car out of mission funds. This story is not untypical, and as you can imagine this attitude did not sit comfortably with the careful economy of the mission culture, where resources were so short and the need always so great.

The Native Church Constitution and leadership training were key tools to encourage native church leadership and ultimately an independent native church. To John this was a priority, but the Bishop thought in bigger sweeps than that. Going through the detail of a constitution was not what he naturally focused on, but rather on the bigger gestures – on bringing people in and expanding the work. Later, when he went to Britain for the Lambeth conference in 1930, he succeeded in raising £16,000 in the few months that he was there.

This is not to say that John's relationship with the Bishop was not a good one; they were both very mature and gracious people who wanted the same thing, the growth and maturing of the Tanganyikan church. The Bishop held John in enormous respect and never sought to promote anybody above him or to undermine him in any way. In return, John knew his place and that much of what the Bishop brought to the Diocese, the enthusiasm and interest and resources, were things he had long dreamed of. The relationship of Secretary and Bishop was central to everything that happened in the Diocese, and only out of a good quality relationship could good quality work come.

The Diocese now had the benefit of Dr Buntine who recommended that a hospital should be built at Kilimatindi, to the west and appeals were made for supplies for this hospital. Then in mid 1929 Dr Wallace arrived, a Jamaican of mixed African and Indian descent. He went on to found a leper colony near Kilimatindi so once again Mvumi was overlooked as a suitable place for developing medical work.

Miss Jackson's annual letter, written in July 1929, describes more of the changes this influx of newcomers was making.

> Mr Lousada has started weekend visits by lorry to the Out Schools, taking Communion to the isolated Christians, and stirring up teachers, often discouraged and even careless about their work. The lorry is used for building during the week. These visits to Out Schools, leaving one day and returning the next, are wonderful to us, who have been accustomed to a week being spent in getting to, and returning from these more distant places. The teachers assemble at the head station, for two days, once a month, they see the work of the Station School, and receive teaching themselves, and lately we have started a time of discussion among themselves about their work. One had been reproved for his mistaken way of forcing attendance at school, alienating children and parents. He was advised to pray more, and he answered, 'If you see a lion coming to attack you, do you stand still and pray? Don't you run away to save yourself?' Another answered him by showing him the way he should help himself, together with prayer, first making friends with the parents and showing them the love and goodness that is in Christianity, as a means of leading them to Christ Himself. Later on the same man thought it necessary to add to his advice, and to tell those who went to make friends with the heathen to be strong in Christ, and not to be dragged back by them into beer drinking and other excesses.

'Mvumi: A Beacon' was how Bishop Chambers headed a piece in his Diocesan Letter for August 1930. 'Here is what might be called the central station of the whole mission, where Conferences are held and Archdeacon Briggs lives. Everybody likes Mvumi'.

However, the dispensary accommodation was deteriorating and contrasted poorly with the new school buildings. Bishop

Chambers included a long article from Miss Thornton in his Letter in which she took up Miss Forsythe's long held theme. He put it under the title

A NEW HOSPITAL NEEDED AT MVUMI, NEAR DODOMA

The present Hospital consists of two small rooms, one more like a cupboard, the larger taking with difficulty three narrow canvas stretchers. My native nurse, Sechelela, sleeps in the small one unless there is an infectious patient. The furniture consists of two stools, a cupboard, and a linen –press made out of packing cases, two worn-out baskets serve as cribs, standing on stools. There is one piece of rubber sheeting, and I made several pillows of unbleached calico and packing from round china. Mattresses are not used. The linen-press contains the treasured store of sheets and towels, all practically worn out, and still well patched, sheets sent out as old linen being used before being finally used as dressings.

The dispensary consists of two small rooms, one a waiting room, hopelessly inadequate, as thirty to seventy people call each day with various complaints. The infant mortality is appalling; each mother seems to have had ten or twelve children, and yet only two or three are living; the children die from unknown complaints at walking age.

There were over 12,000 attendances last year. The records of patients during the afternoons, evenings and nights I did not try to keep. There were 50 cases in hospital, many being refused through lack of room. Other attendances are bull-ants, which come in in swarms, and make holes for the snakes, some of which, large and very deadly, have been killed inside and outside the hospital.

This brings our heartfelt thanks for all you have sent. The greatness of your help you will never realise unless you came and saw things with your own eyes. The people have so very, very little, one feels ashamed that one ever grumbled about any condition or circumstance in all one's life. Sechelela was delighted with everything, wanting to know who gave them. The patients do appreciate help. In readiness for the day when we shall have a hospital and a doctor of our own, with proper equipment, we treasure everything to that end. Two or three enamel dishes came in one of the boxes, and Sechelela ran off with them and hid them so quickly, mumbling something about the new hospital, that I haven't yet been able to find them.

WHAT £150 WOULD DO

Isn't there another doctor like Dr Buntine who would like to come? He would never regret it, whoever he might be, it's too interesting and too great a work to ever have regrets about. Oh, I wish I had a lot of money to build my own hospital. They tell me £150 will build three rooms at a time. Can't someone leave that amount to us for a hospital? Ours is really crumbling to pieces.

A hospital for Mvumi was one of the many things on Bishop Chambers shopping list as he visited England for Lambeth in 1930 and this moving first hand plea was part of his effective campaigning.

At the end of the rainy season early in 1930 the new girls school buildings suffered severely. John cabled the Bishop 'Cyclone unroofed nearly all boarding school Mvumi today'. It left only the Common Room with any remaining cover. The courtyards were a foot deep in water and the roofless rooms were like pools, with everything including all the food left standing in the water. Resources were so valuable and so hard won that such events were a considerable set back. John told the Bishop that peoples' houses were falling down with the heavy rain and so he was housing about 50 people. 'I am seriously thinking of trying to raise the money somehow to put an iron roof over my Church before the next rainy season. Several tons of corrugated iron would be very acceptable out here!'

Child mortality in 1930 was still estimated to be 80%. The girls at Mvumi Girls Boarding School were trained in a wide variety of subjects besides the academic subjects, amongst which were mothercraft, infant welfare, and home nursing of the sick. The girls lived in dormitory 'families' who had various responsibilities between them. The school adopted a few orphaned infants and young children with troubled backgrounds. These children were brought up in these families, and so the girls were given first hand experience of healthy care for young children. A study* of Mvumi old girls that was done many years later found that the child mortality experienced in their families as they went on to be mothers was 20%, and in some cases old girls had not lost any of their children at all.

The girls were also given practical nursing experience in the dispensary under the supervision of Miss Thornton, and so were the beginnings of nurse training at Mvumi. Narelle Bullard, also a nurse, visited for Christmas and wrote in her letters home 'Miss Thornton has lots of work here and how she manages in her poky clinic I don't know but some day she is going to have a very swish place and they hope some of the girls will train there from the school.'

There had been a General Conference of native leaders and missionaries at Mvumi in September of 1930, to discuss issues of church management and practice. One of the subjects discussed at this meeting was on the baptism of polygamists. The minutes record:

> The Conference carefully considered the question of a polyga-mist putting away his wives in order that he might be baptised. This was deprecated and Conference considered it preferable for a Polygamist to stay in the Catechumenate or an unbaptised man rather than that any of his wives for whom he had accepted responsibility should be put away.

The Conference went even further, and asked the Bishop to consider the question of bringing polygamists into fuller fellow-ship with the rest of the church. It is easy to see how important it was that the practices of the growing new church should be formed and shaped by its own native leaders as well as the foreign missionary.

Another item discussed at that Conference was the collecting together of all existing choruses, both in Cigogo and in Swahili. The choruses were then to be published in a small book. This might seem like a matter of no consequence, but collecting

---

* Quoted in Avis Richardson's memoirs of the school, 'Hold High the Torch' p. 153

together and publishing the songs that had been written here and there, and sharing them with other parts of the church was encouraging the existing native talent and inclination to improvise songs.

Out of this collaboration of native ways and Christian teaching came something quite new as far as the mission was concerned. If there was sufficient harvest then in July each year the initiation rites of young people take place. These involve circumcision camps out in the bush alongside teaching, which would normally be of traditional content. In the Annual Report of the Mission (1930/31) it describes what they tried:

> We held this year a new type of 'jando' or camp; and without taking away anything that was good in the native custom we have, through chosen camp leaders, introduced cleanliness and instruction which will, we hope bear fruit in the lives of the boys who pass through.

This was radical action indeed, to take the native customs and adapt them, weaving in Christian teaching in place of witchcraft and superstition.

On 4 June 1931 the Tanganyika Mission became the responsibility of CMS Australia, and all powers held by the CMS committee in London were given to Australia on that date. The relationship was complicated since Australia could not afford to bear the entire financial burden and so those, such as John, whose allowances came from London continued to be paid from there. However, as far as management went, the work was the responsibility of CMS Australia.

Mvumi had become a good place for new recruits; with a considerable number of experienced missionaries there somebody new could come and learn language skills, whilst not being too isolated and lonely in the process. At the same time their health was likely to be better, since they were being looked after, and not too much was being asked of them in their initial year or two as they learnt the language. So in 1931 Miss Thornton in turn was transferred to Buigiri and newly arrived Nurse May Dobson was appointed to the Mvumi Dispensary.

Mvumi hosted a meeting of the missionaries Executive Committee on 30–31 December 1931 who recorded 'great regret at the absence of the Archdeacon through illness, and appreciates greatly the kind hospitality so generously given them by him and Mrs Briggs, and hopes that the Archdeacon will soon be restored to his usual health and vigour'. The Executive Committee also 'places on record its appreciation of the special efforts of Native congregations to attain self-support during this coming year, notably at Mvumi and Buigiri'. Quite a milestone reached.

Kiboriani was not being used as extensively as it had been in earlier years. It was not big enough to accommodate the bigger meetings and since transport was now by road rather than with porters, other places were easier to get to. Kiboriani was at the top of a mountain range. The Executive Committee was concerned at its decline; its upkeep cost money and there were certainly health benefits to taking holidays at an altitude that was beyond the reach of malarial mosquitoes. All the missionaries were told that it was preferred that they should take their holidays there. They also resolved to make more use of it for Conventions and Conferences.

Mvumi Girls Boarding School had finally been completed and on 24 March 1932 there was a great gathering to recognise this achievement and to dedicate the work there. The service was printed in Cigogo and English. His Excellency, the Governor, Sir G Stewart-Symes (KBE, CMG, DSO) was introduced to the large gathering by Archdeacon Briggs, and he officially opened the school. Chief Mazengo expressed the thanks of his people for the visit of the Governor and Bishop Chambers offered the dedicatory prayer.

> *O Lord Jesus Christ, Son of the Living God, Who art the brightness of the Father's Glory, and the express image of His Person. Bless this school now to be dedicated in Thy Name, and grant that it may ever be a Tabernacle for Thy Truth, a home of learning, and a place of cherished associations in the development of*

Christian character to the Glory of Thy Name,
Who, with the Father and the Holy Spirit, livest and reignest one
God world without end. Amen.
God the Father, God the Son, God the Holy Ghost, accept, hallow
and bless this place to the end whereto we dedicate it this day.
The Lord with His favour graciously regard it and send down
upon it His benediction and grace now and for evermore. Amen

The previous day Governor Sir Stewart-Symes had laid the Foundation Stone of Dodoma Cathedral, a stone which bears the name of the Venerable Archdeacon J H Briggs. What a beautiful honour, and surely not one that John himself would have ever expected. Of the band of pioneering missionaries who he had joined at the age of 24 he really had been amongst the least. Now, forty years later, he was honoured as a central figure in the founding of the new Diocese.

Extracts of a letter from Sister Dobson were published by CMS in March 1932, in it she tells of her experiences.

Sister May Dobson

We have a poor little baby, terribly thin, who was being fed on porridge. I found out it was 6 months old and it only weighs 6 pounds. ...Yes! The work is hard, especially the diagnosing, when you don't know one tropical disease from another. Yet one is wonderfully preserved from making blunders. We find this is so, time after time. The Hospital and Dispensary are not all that could be desired. If you open the front door of either you just about get blown out, and the whole place fills with dust, so it is very difficult to keep anything sterile. I don't know if we can carry on in it very much longer. Miss Thornton says that in the wet weather it is difficult to keep the patients dry, even by standing up all night, and the babies have to be put in a box under the bed for shelter.

The growing worldwide economic depression had inevitable consequences in the Diocese, there was less money available to support the work. In 1930 the budget had been £7,720 for the year, but in 1932 this had to be reduced to £5,000, which, after it had been exchanged was only worth £3,750. The Executive Committee met in April and protested about this severe cut in funding.

> This [amount] it will readily be seen is totally inadequate. By the use of savings from Government Grants, the abolition of medical, dental, holiday travelling and loads allowances to the missionaries, the closing down of outstations, the dismissal of teachers, the curtailment of itineration and the consequent less frequent supervision of native workers and the lessening of evangelistic effort, the neglect of repairs to mission property, and the throwing of additional burdens on missionaries, it has been found possible to save £750 this year. ... We can see no other alternative but the withdrawal of workers.

A letter from Miss Jackson was published in the CMS magazine, the Gleaner, in April: 'Yesterday the Archdeacon called a meeting of all the Christians to discuss the financial situation. A large number promised regular donations, which should be a great help. I can hear a cow and calf, the first contribution to arrive.'

The educational grants from Government also became harder to get. In June 1932 Bishop Chambers wrote to CMS Australia saying 'I am sorry we cannot find the full CMS allowance for Avis Richardson. But in the absence of a grant we feel we could provide her with her maintenance of £30 a year, and even with a grant this is all that is really provided.' Avis Richardson was a teacher hoping to join the staff at Mvumi Girls School, she was to be an invaluable and long-serving member of the Mvumi staff. She finally left Australia on 9 October 1932 and in her beautifully written memoir

'Hold High the Torch', she describes the culmination of her long awaited journey.

> We took our places in sleeping compartments on the train for our trip through unknown country. Mine was to be the longest, over 300 miles. The train was slow and at every station there was a 20 minute or so wait, and then the wood burning engine would blow its big whistle and we would continue our east-west journey, through the night. ... I arrived in daylight and was met by Archdeacon Briggs and warmly welcomed.

Pressure came to bear on the Diocese to retire the most senior missionaries at the end of their present tour of service. This included John Briggs, who by this time was 64 years old. The Executive Committee pleaded strongly for the retention of Archdeacon Briggs, because of his special gifts in the administration and conservation of missionary funds. In other words he would earn his keep with his careful management and savings. John wrote to CMS in London, suggesting that they just pay him his pension and continue to pay for his passage home when needed, but that Australia would make up the difference of allowances.

> With the Bishop's policy of developing the Native Ministry and leadership I feel I can be especially helpful through my knowledge of the language and local conditions. The Diocese is such an infant at present and with the new Constitution to work out I feel I have a contribution to make as a completion of my life work in Tanganyika.

This plea was accepted and John and Annie were able to stay. Even the Government was struggling to pay the mission what had already been promised. They had promised Mvumi Girls Boarding School maintenance grants for 43 of the girls, but these were withheld because of shortage of funds.

The decision-making process in the Diocese was continuing to evolve. In the few days preceding the Executive Committee meeting in April, there had been a Central Church Council meeting, at which the Bishop, John and one or two other missionaries had met with the senior native church leaders, such as Haruni Mbega, Andrea Mwaka, Daudi Mhando, and, amongst others, the Mvumi delegates Danieli Calo and Danieli Mghambi. The discussions and opinions expressed and decisions made could then be fed into the exclusively missionary Executive Committee meeting. This was a gradual closing of the gap, and a progression towards one body made up of senior missionary leaders and senior native leaders that would govern the work of the Diocese, the Diocesan Council.

On 29 June Mika Muloli and Danyeli Mbogo were ordained as deacons at St Peters church, Mvumi. This was part of a wider movement, as the Bishop reported in his Diocesan Letter in August 1932. He had ordained five men in total, each in their local areas in order to build their position of leadership among their own people. He wrote:

> The actual ordination services were times of great blessing, I feel sure, to all present. The churches were crowded. Intense interest was shown everywhere. It was to be seen quite plainly that the people recognised that big things were happening in their midst, when one of their number, called of God, was receiving the commission of Christ in the Apostolic ministry. Mazengo and another chief were present at Mvumi, where the service had to be specially translated into Cigogo. I used a typewritten copy, thus bringing home to us the need of releasing one of our older missionaries for translational work.

The Diocese still did not have a complete published translation of the Bible in Cigogo. How could native church leaders develop and grow if they did not have access to the entire Bible in their own language? As the church leadership grew this need became more pressing. Thirty years before, Westgate, Doulton and Briggs had all worked hard to produce translations of the Old Testament books which were of sufficient quality and accuracy for publication. These had all been lost during the destruction of mission property by the Germans during the First World War and other needs in the years since had prevented much whole-sale tackling of the problem. The amount of work involved in accurate translation is huge. The work cannot be done solely by one person, but should be done as a team, so that checks can be made on the slant a particular word might give, and to improve accuracy and clarity. The work can only be done by those with superb language skills and fluency, and knowledge and understanding of the colloquial use of the language. It involves people being set aside from other duties and being able to dedicate themselves to the translation for extended periods of time. And of course, just as the Bishop knew so well, the most valuable people to assist him in the everyday running of the Diocese were the same people who would need to be set aside if the translation was to be done. Could John ever be spared?

Miss Jackson was faithfully soldiering on. The village school she had been in charge of for so many years was now run by native teachers. Ten more of the teachers were studying at Kongwa to improve their teaching skills. Miss Jackson was able to concentrate her efforts on those who had often been neglected, the outschool teachers. Despite her growing age and infirmity she went camping around the area during the dry season. She stayed at the different places where they were living, and tried to lead them by example. She also continued her pattern of taking them away from their work on a monthly basis, as described in her Annual Letter for 1932:

> The teachers from the outstations come to the head station at the beginning of each month for two days, as they have been doing for years, and their wants are supplied as far as possible, and their spiritual needs are brought to the Provider of all. We trust they go back to their work renewed and strengthened. They are the ones on whom depend the extension of Christ's kingdom in the land. A large proportion of the baptisms are the result of their work. They also carry on bush schools, which are the beginning of the children's education.

In November 1933 a remarkable conference was held at Mvumi at the instigation of Bishop Chambers. It was a drawing together of all those missions working in the region, Germans, Americans, Swedes, Danes, Czechoslovakians as well as Australians and British and it was concerned with the development of a

United Church for Central Africa. It was thought to be a very important meeting and Avis Richardson, who had been a secretary and book-keeper before becoming a teacher, was called upon to take down what was said. She wrote about the event later.

> The vision of one United Church for all Central Africa gripped all and I realised as never before the richness of blessing that could come from one United Church, all the different missions bringing their wealth of spiritual experience. The object of seeking for a United Church was to build up on the best possible foundation the Church that would have to be handed over to the Africans themselves some time in the future and it would need to be a strong Church.

Sadly the Union didn't happen, because the high Anglican society, UMCA, and the other protestant societies could not accept each other, the gulf being too wide. What a different story the Tanganyikan church might have told had events taken a different turn here.

Sister Dobson described her developing medical work; they were seeing an average of 1200 patients a month, and 'the inpatient work has been made easier by the building of a new ward for maternity cases'. She wrote:

> There have been several changes in the native staff and an attempt is now being made to train girls who have just left school. Some of the girls from the Boarding School are helping also, through going to the dispensary each morning.

Miss Jackson had suffered a stroke at some point earlier, people remember that she had become weak on one side, but she had carried on as ever. At the end of 1933 she had another more serious stroke and the nursing care she needed brought a halt to much other work. The school had broken up in early December, but as Avis Richardson wrote:

> We were unable, however, to open again at the time we expected because of the very serious illness of Miss Effie Jackson. ... So

serious was her illness that she had to be watched all day and all night for some time, and that meant that every member of staff on that mission station had to share in that task.

The senior native women whom she knew best and who had worked closely with her for many years also shared in her care. Miss Jackson's nursing care continued through January, as her health gradually sank, until she died on 1 February 1934, aged about 55 years old. Her death was a great loss to the Mvumi community, her home for 25 years. It was also a great loss to the outstation teachers who she had supported and encouraged for so long, and to John Briggs who had depended on her and on the quality and consistency of her work for all those years. She had been a quiet devoted teacher of the people, and she was still remembered clearly in 1999. When I asked the very elderly Lazaro Ndajilo about her, his wizened lean face and near sightless eyes lit up with the brightness of full sunshine, and he said 'oh, Bibi Jackson, Mama yetu, aliwasha taa hapa' (Oh, Miss Jackson, our Mother, she lit the lamp here). She is remembered as someone who drew people to her with love; she was very patient, and even when someone had wronged her she didn't get angry. She was interested in people and in their work and welcomed people if they came to her. Those who knew her could visit her at any time and go to her without fear. She was also very musical, playing the piano in church and always singing with people. Bishop Chambers described her as 'a gentle quiet woman of God, esteemed and loved'.

It is remembered that John never visited Miss Jackson in her final illness, and that she lamented this. I can only imagine that he was so stricken with sadness and grief that he could not trust himself or his emotions to face her. He did not report her death to CMS until 3 weeks later, on the 22 February, when he wrote 'this station suffered a great loss in the death of Miss Effie Emily Jackson, a Missionary of the New South Wales Branch, Australia, through a paralytic stroke. We thank God for the splendid work done on this station by this veteran missionary.' When he preached at her funeral, about her life and work, it is remembered that he cried. She was buried in the small old graveyard next to the infant son of John and Violet Briggs, along with so many friends such as Andreya Lungwa.

In the New Years Honours list published at the very end of 1934, John Henry Briggs was awarded the OBE, another honour I am sure he never dreamed of. At some point in 1935 Sir Harold MacMichael stopped off on a journey through Dodoma and the train waited while he presented John with his medal in a simple ceremony held on the platform of Dodoma station. The picture shows very few witnesses to the occasion, but a proud Mrs Briggs standing shaded from the sun under an umbrella and a humble but honoured Archdeacon.

Archdeacon John H Briggs receiving his OBE
Courtesy CMS

Angelina Reed, a visitor to Mvumi at this time, gave the following description of Mvumi and paints a vivid picture of John and Annie:

This was where Archdeacon and Mrs Briggs lived in much happiness with two other missionaries, a nurse and a secretary. The mission included a modern African Girls' Boarding School, with four European teachers, all of whom seemed to work about 16 or more hours per day. They arranged their own timetable and all worked supremely happily together, looking upon Archdeacon and Mrs Briggs as their Father and Mother. ... The Archdeacon apparently never did things by halves and was a good organizer. He cultivated a well-stocked garden, about a mile from the house, where water was readily obtained by digging a short distance below the surface so there were many refreshing wells and fruit trees in abundance; banana palms, orange and lemon trees, mango and pomegranate trees; grape vines, pineapples, passion fruit etc etc and pawpaws of various varieties. When staying at Mvumi there was generally five kinds of fruit to choose from at breakfast time. ... To step from the dry parched earth into this garden was a paradise indeed, and reminded me of the Garden of Eden. There was a bower of pink roses as one entered the garden gate and so on all through the garden.

John had a grandfatherly air:

I think it was the way he carved a joint, as well as the way he provided for his big family.

Avis Richardson paints a similar picture:

My arrival at Mvumi was memorable. I was very warmly welcomed by Mrs Briggs .. Visitors often came to that mission station from Dodoma, and Mrs Briggs, a delightful, gracious lady, was always a welcoming and very hospitable hostess, her husband sharing with her in that warmth of welcome and hospitality. Later I was to live with them for nine months, a very happy memory. In that

Avis Richardson

land of far apart centres, if anyone among our missionaries was ill, it was a great boon to them to be taken into the home of Archdeacon and Mrs Briggs and be nursed back to health and ability to travel.

Avis and the other younger missionaries had a lot to learn from John's long years of experience. She wrote 'The Archdeacon ... told us all sorts of stories. He was most interesting when he just sat down and talked to us of his experiences during the 40 years that he had been in that country.'

Narelle Bullard's letters

Mr Briggs is a dear – I had a good old bust up with him over my work and in the end he said 'well do as you like'. He fathers us all and when he is here I nearly burst after meals, he makes us take all he gives and gets very annoyed if we don't eat it. He brought a load of meat and a load of bread ... On Saturday afternoon Mr Briggs had to drive to Kikombo to send a communion set to Mr Cordell ... so he took sister and I for a spin ... I did enjoy that spin.

Building work had continued at Mvumi and the memoirs of Avis Richardson are descriptive:

By the end of 1934 a new hospital had been built, not far from our big playground to the west. The old building of wood and mud had become far too small and entirely inadequate for the growing work. Archdeacon Briggs was the architect and builder of the new wards and all the effort he put into building and equipping them was amply repaid by the tremendous increase in maternity cases. One very large new ward was for maternity cases and another building the same size consisted of two wards, one women's general and the other for children. A third new building was used by the hospital staff and trainees. An older building on the same site continued to be used as a men's ward, until another new ward was built.

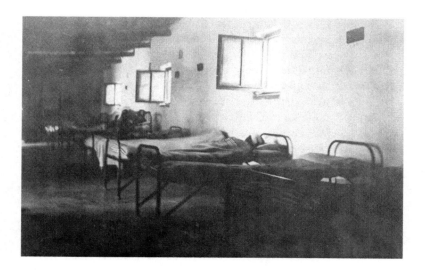

The new Hospital quadrangle and wards

It took quite a long time to break down opposition where maternity work was concerned. The old Wagogo midwives did all they could to hinder women going to a European hospital to have their babies and their influence was surprisingly strong. The younger women often feared to go against their wishes. The Mission was very keen for as many cases as possible to go to their maternity clinics because infant mortality was so high, 75%, often higher in some families. I remember asking our housemaid, Esteri, how many babies she had had. She replied, 'I have had ten babies, but only Stanley is alive.

It was extraordinarily difficult to make a woman understand the right way to feed a little baby. The babies died mainly from wrong feeding, thick gruel was rammed down their throats by the mother's fingers until they bulged sufficiently to satisfy the mother that the baby had really been fed! There were instances too with regard to mother's milk in some areas, when a witchdoctor would tell a mother she must not feed her baby from one of her breasts, but use only the other.

If mothers could be persuaded to go into the hospital, they received antenatal treatment every week and after the babies were born they could bring them in every Monday to be weighed and receive advice as to how to feed them. The Chief, Mazengo, took a keen interest in the medical work at Mvumi and recognised the immense value of the maternity and child welfare centre to his people, with the result that he ordered all the women in his district to go to the hospital for treatment, threatening them with a fine of ten shillings each if they did not go. The fee at the hospital was one shilling. At that time a man's daily wage in a labouring capacity was thirty cents and there were one hundred cents in a shilling.

Up to the previous July, seven had been the record number of babies born in one month at our clinic, and in that month twenty three were born. We were tremendously excited at such a phenomenon. That was the record until the end of the year but immediately the new hospital was ready for use, the number went up. The chief sent out to numbers of villages and ordered expectant mothers to the hospital and scores of them came in to be 'written down', which meant that they were to visit the hospital every week for treatment and advice till the baby was born. As a result a record was created every month. In January 50 were born, in February 57, in March 74, in April 80 and in May 86. This was really remarkable.

A few weeks after the new building was opened, the maternity ward was filled to capacity and the overflow had to go into the women's general ward. Bonny, healthy babies were being born constantly. Sister Dobson was in charge of the hospital and was the only European there. She was due for furlough, but because of the tremendous shortage of nurses in the Mission, she had to wait another year till a nurse returned from home leave. A second nurse was badly needed now to help share the responsibility of such a big work. The African staff were good, but needed constant supervision in those days to prevent slackness. It consisted of Secelela, an older African woman – her name meant rejoicing – who had had years of experience in medical work, and seven girls (six of whom were ex-Mvumi schoolgirls) some fully trained and the rest still being trained. Two years earlier Miss Dobson had been called for every case day and night. Secelela would not attempt anything on her own.

As time went on, however, the staff had gone so far ahead that the trained girls took every normal case and would only call Secelela if a case proved to be abnormal, and if she found it really too difficult, only then did she call Miss Dobson. If Miss Dobson could not trust her staff, it would be quite impossible to carry on the hospital. There had been occasions when five babies were born in the one night.

At that time they were facing the difficulty of finding more helpers. Four more at least were needed then and we had asked all the older suitable girls in the school if any of them would be willing to go to the hospital for training and all had refused for various reasons, some because the parents very strongly objected. ... It was the age-old custom with them for the old women of the tribe to be the midwives and it was this that caused them to give us an unhesitating and emphatic refusal. Another difficulty was the early marrying age of the girls in that area.

At last the health issues that Miss Forsythe had long seen, and cried out to be able to do a bit more about, were being given a place of more importance. In April 1935 the hospital held a Child Welfare and Health Week with extensive involvement from the whole mission community and drawing people in from far and wide. Avis Richardson again gives a beautiful description of the event.

Preparations were made for weeks beforehand and the event was widely advertised throughout the whole district, so that all who were able would be attracted to come in and they did. The response was splendid.

The week began on Sunday, when sermons were preached concerning health from the Christian standpoint. Every morning during the week following, lectures and demonstrations were given, one section being carried out by members of our school mothercraft class to show the correct way to wean a baby. This was a tremendously important teaching there and needed to be hammered in again and again. Mothers did not realise how they endangered their babies' lives through wrong feeding, thinking it quite all right to take a child straight from milk food and give it solid 'wugali'. The girls were most interested and enthusiastically prepared each day the various thicknesses of gruel required for each stage. Everything was done in native vessels and lecturettes given from time to time by the girls who had prepared them.

On another table nearly all manner of locally procurable foods were displayed, grouped according to their type to show food values, and lecturettes were given on the subject by the hospital trainees.

On Monday afternoon health plays were staged in the school common-room, and these drew big crowds. So many came, including Chief Mazengo and other chiefs with their retinues, that two sessions had to be arranged, the women first and then the men. During the first session the babies howled and the women talked and it was most difficult to get reasonable quietness. Obedience and self-control were most difficult lessons for these people to learn and we too find it an equally difficult lesson for us to learn to practise patience at all times! The girls who went to the hospital to help in the out-patients' department, acted in the plays. In all, these little plays were put on five times during the week and Chief Mazengo was so interested that he wanted them put on yet again on Saturday afternoon for all the chiefs he intended bringing with him that day, which was to be the day of days. The chiefs came, but Saturday's events excluded the possibility of putting on the plays again.

Ten little girls in the school put on a tableau as an item of interest to show how babies were carried in different parts of the world ... Two lantern lectures were held at night, showing medical slides, the emphasis being on flies and the harm they can cause.

Lectures were given daily by Sister May Dobson to large audiences of women, and one afternoon Archdeacon Briggs lectured the men to make them realise their responsibility in family life where the health of the mother and children were concerned.

Several competitions, which were held during the week, created great interest. One was a cot-making competition, in which the fathers took part. They had to make a cot suitable for use in a Cigogo 'kaya', of materials obtainable locally. Some very nice cots were produced and some showed quite a lot of originality. Some competitors made provision for the fixing of a mosquito net on the cot. Mosquito nets were available in Dodoma and we wanted to make their use popular, as malaria plays havoc among the people. This idea was introduced into one of the health plays too.

The women had a cooking competion, 'wugali' and 'wubaga' (gruel). A large number entered for it and the numerous pots were placed in rows down the whole length of one of the long verandahs. The judging of the exhibits was most amusing. Four Wagogo women were the judges – Canon Andrea Mwaka's wife was one, and the Rev Mika Muloli's wife was another. They had a right royal time tasting the contents of every pot and showing that the proof was in the eating. Some of us were waiting expectantly to see what would happen about a certain pot of most attractive looking 'wubaga'. It was smooth and creamy, and looked delicious. To our surprise no comment was made when they tasted it, so after a little while we drew their attention to the pot. Secelela was near and tasted it, and screwed up her nose. Then Marita Mwaka tasted it again and she too screwed up her nose, saying disdainfully 'There is cows fat and sugar in it!' the proof was in the eating there all right!

The event was also described in full in the Church Missionary Gleaner, by a mystery missionary from Mvumi, who records the event with the eyes of a newcomer.

Saturday, the closing day, was the biggest of all, and the day of the actual Baby Show. People began to arrive from villages many miles away, even as early as 8 o'clock in the morning. They must have got up while it was still dark. Mazengo, the Chief of the Mvumi district, accompanied by four other chiefs of surrounding districts, and many of the headmen from each district, arrived during the morning, and a huge crowd gradually gathered. By 11 o'clock (when we were expecting the Provincial Commissioner from Dodoma, and other government officials..) the Mission was just black with people, and as the Commissioner's car drove up they ranged themselves into two lines, and cheered as he drove through this guard of honour. ... Indeed a very happy spirit prevailed throughout the day, and although many of the mothers who had brought babies to the show had stood about in the sun for a considerable time, they were all laughing and happy; Africa loves a crowd!

The first item on the programme for the afternoon was the official opening of the new hospital by the Provincial Commissioner, and then a tour of inspection. This was followed by a procession of children, ranging from six years old to one month, the young ones, of course, having to be carried by their mothers. Nearly five hundred babies were present. At the beginning of each section a banner was carried denoting how old the children were, and then after this each group was led to a different shady spot ready for the judging. The judges had a very busy time with the hundreds of children who entered in the various age groups. It soon became easy, though, to find those whose mothers had profited by teaching, for their children were outstanding in every way – clean and well kept, healthy and well fed, but not over fed. There were no bad eyes with them – one of Africa's greatest troubles amongst babies. Eyes get bad, and are left, and there are so many flies about. With ordinary care, though, the babies can be healthy, and most of the mothers are extremely anxious to learn. The judging was followed by the prize-giving, and many happy faces were seen as the chosen ones came up to receive their prizes, which were given out by Chief Mazengo.

So one simple sentence describes the birth of Mvumi Hospital, one prayed for and awaited for so many years. On Saturday 13 April 1935 Mr Hignell, the Provincial Commissioner, came to Mvumi to open the new hospital. He was accompanied by the District Officer who spoke very nicely at the ceremony too. More than that I don't know. It must have been a brief ceremony with so much else happening that day, but the old friends Archdeacon Briggs and Chief Mazengo would also have had a part to play.

Opposition was never far away. Avis Richardson describes what happened next.

> Just after the Child Welfare and Health Week, Miss May Dobson went away on annual leave and then some old women arrived at the hospital and told the women waiting there that the month of June that year was an evil month and that no babies would be born at all during that time, and that therefore it was of no use their waiting on at the hospital. Such a story could do a lot of harm, but the Archdeacon went up and calmed the women's fears, telling them that there was no curse on the hospital, and that all would be well.

Only months after the opening of the hospital Miss Richardson described the arrival of 'an honoured patient, Canon Andrea Mwaka, the dearly loved saintly Canon of Dodoma Cathedral'. She continued the account:

Andrea Mwaka
Courtesy CMS

To our sorrow he passed away one Saturday night, but we would not call him back, because to have recovered from his illness would have meant for him a life of constant pain. He has given the very best years of his life to Christ's service, having taken up his work as a Christian teacher 53 years ago.

He had been ill in Dodoma for some considerable time before coming to Mvumi ... He commented when he came that when one is about to die, he likes to be among his own people and also he wanted Marita, his wife, to be among her friends. He was always most thoughtful for her. Not long before, he said that during all the years of their married life he and his wife had never quarrelled once, a most unusual thing for an African to be able to say. So often we heard of quarrelling

between husbands and wives, and wife-beating, especially when
plenty of beer was about, as it was after the harvests had been
gathered and beer was always made then.

Canon Andrea had a face that radiated joy, peace and goodness, and to know him was to love him. His own people loved and
revered him as a man above his fellows. As a Mugogo said the
day after he died 'All the countryside has sorrow because of his
passing.'

The funeral took place on Sunday evening at about sunset.
The Service for the Burial of the Dead was held in the church, a
large number of people present, and just after it had begun the
Rev. G. A. Conolly arrived and was able to help the Rev. Mika
Muloli, who had had an exceptionally long and tiring day, having
taken the usual Sunday morning services, one a big Holy
Communion Service, the funeral and looking after Chief
Mazengo, who had come for the funeral. After the service the
Rev. George Conolly and the Rev. Mika Muloli led the way to the
cemetery, followed by teachers carrying the coffin.

In the meantime all of our schoolgirls and the village school
children had lined up outside the cemetery to form a guard of
honour and as the cortage [sic] turned the corner at the hospital
and came in sight, the children began to sing a hymn, 'The happy
morn has come'. It was truly impressive to us who were
approaching. During the whole time that the service was being
held at the church and again at the cemetery, the drum was being
beaten, the solemn strange beating of the drum used only when a
chief dies – a few slow beats, a few rapid beats, sudden silence for
a space, then the same again. Canon Andrea was truly a chief
amongst his people.

The training work going on in the hospital was progressing
rapidly and Avis Richardson's memoirs contain a lengthy
description of one such great step forward:

One of the outstanding events of the first term in 1936, was pres-
entation of a certificate for the Maternity and Child Welfare
work done by Blandina, an ex-student of ours, who became one
of the first trainees at the Mvumi Hospital. Blandina, in her
childhood, was left in the care of heathen relatives, while her
father was doing the work of a dresser for a mission elsewhere.
She wanted to come to school, but her relatives would not permit

it. Her father, returning to Mvumi, found that his daughter was in danger while living with those people, so he brought her along to school, at the age of thirteen years. Though anxious to learn, she did not find lessons easy, but she did learn to read and write.

During the holidays she stayed at the Mvumi School and looked after the two school babies, receiving wages for her work. Her father, having lost his position, came along regularly and took possession of all she earned, much to her disgust.

She proved so faithful and capable in her work of looking after the children that she was regarded as a possible trainee for the hospital. She very willingly agreed to the suggestion, saying 'now my father will not be able to come and take all my wages'. She was to receive only 1/- a month and her keep.

She had ups and downs during her time of training, but she came through well and in due course was a very reliable and capable maternity nurse. Her marriage to Mika Salali, one of the village school teachers, took place, but she did not sever entirely her connection with the hospital.

Several new trainees began that year and Blandina went every day from early morning till midday to supervise their work and guide them. She rejoiced so much at having that responsible work.

Her Certificate was presented to her in the presence of a large gathering in the school assembly hall. Archdeacon Briggs, Dr Wallace, Chief Mazengo, the Rev Mika Muloli and the Rev Elieza Lemanya were on the platform and the Archdeacon presented the Certificate. It was a very important occasion as Blandina was the first Mugogo woman to receive such a Certificate. Speeches were made by nearly all on the platform, stressing the importance and tremendous value of the work, and pointing out to the girls present the opportunity for service to God awaiting those who would be willing to be trained in the hospital. We were delighted that as a result of that gathering four girls offered for service in the hospital.

Even in the mid 1930's soil erosion was raising its head as a problem for the Mvumi area. A government agricultural officer set up camp for two months near the river with nine trained African instructors. As the land had become more travelled by cattle, these tracks became rivers in the rains and much of the topsoil had been washed away. This had meant that people had

had to give up cultivating near the river as the soil was not good enough. Chief Mazengo had to provide one hundred men for ten days who worked under the instructors with the Agricultural Officer supervising. After ten days an ox was killed and they had a feast. Then another hundred men started work. Levels were marked out and then with the help of crowbars and shovels the men dug trenches six to eight feet wide and about a foot deep. They formed mounds one and a half feet high on the lower side, and again about six to eight feet wide. Grass was to be grown on the mounds and trees to be planted in the trenches. There was grumbling amongst some local people who felt that the country was being ruined but Miss Taylor, headmistress at the Girls School, invited the Agricultural Officer to give a lecture on soil erosion and on anti-erosion methods. She invited the teachers, senior boys of the village school, hospital dressers and mission staff, as well as the school girls, and they tried to practise in their own gardens some of the things they had learnt.

On 14 August 1936 there was a missionaries conference at which several papers were read, including one by Archdeacon John Briggs. We only have the title of John's paper now, 'What do the Africans think of us?' but wouldn't it be interesting to know what he said. No missionary was as well placed as he was to know and appreciate much of what the native people thought, and what was important to them. He had lived in close contact and a dependence on them since the day he landed at Saadani, 44 years before. Along with Bishop Chambers' drive to expand the work of the Diocese had come a large increase in the ranks of missionaries. This wave of new recruits were naturally not as well versed in native thinking nor were they dependent in quite the same way as John had been, so it was surely the case that they made plenty of mistakes, and in some cases held rather one sided views. John's paper was an antidote to this, to encourage these new missionaries to see themselves from an African point of view.

Soon after the hospital buildings were built local people remember that Archdeacon Briggs built an orphanage at the hospital, referred to as 'mdube'. Andrea Mwaka's widow was the first house mother.

The conference was followed a few days later by a two day Diocesan Council meeting; only a few years before, the Diocesan Council meeting came first and fed into the missionaries executive group. Now the missionaries were meeting first and feeding into the Diocesan Council. The minutes record an intention to locate a second nurse at Mvumi, in order to intensify the training of African maternity workers. Sister Banks, the sister of Ralph Banks, who was a nurse working in the west of the Diocese was to be relocated to Mvumi at the end of the year. John reported that the remittances from Australia were insufficient and that unless a further substantial remittance was received in the next fortnight then August salaries could not be paid. The constant juggling of money that he had to do to keep the work of the Diocese on the road was never ending.

In the same year there was an evangelistic mission, and Miss Richardson once again gave a beautiful description:

> Much discussion had taken place about the big mission that was to take place in our district. Outstation teachers came in for their usual monthly teaching and Miss Gelding discussed with them the programme for the Mission taking place for the week from September 15th to the 22nd. Each one had been expected to keep the matter well before the Christians in his district and to arrange for them to go out in groups to heathen villages.
>
> Miss Gelding had arranged to give a series of lantern lectures and intended during that month and part of October to go every Wednesday and Friday evening to various centres to give those lectures. I looked forward tremendously to that, as she planned to take me with her to operate the lantern, and at the same time I would see something of outstations that I had not yet visited.
>
> Our first visit was to the village where Chief Mazengo lived, ten miles away and we showed the pictures at the court house there. We had some splendid slides of the life of Christ, and Miss Gelding had given much thought to whether or not she would use some slides of Bunyan's Pilgrim's Progress. This book had been translated into Kiswahili and contained pictures of Africans acting the story. It was an excellent translation and its value added to by having an excellent set of slides showing the Africans in the story.

Miss Gelding wrote from Mvumi 'we have truly seen the African Church in Action ... In the six days 700 were reached quite close to Mvumi; 500 of them came to church yesterday. The Bishop says "All our African clergy are rising to our expectations of them".' Deaconess Betteridge, also stationed at Mvumi, wrote 'We've had a wonderful awakening amongst our people'.

CMS Australia published a letter from Avis Richardson, writing of the Girls School.

> Last Saturday was sports and prize-giving day, and twenty-seven Europeans from Dodoma, including the Bishop, came out to see the events ... The children were splendid in all their demonstrations. We had a handiwork exhibition of various things made in the school – sisal brooms, head pads, etc etc, and also some examples of darning and patching which appealed tremendously to Chief Mazengo, who said such darning would be a real ornamentation on his clothes. Now he wants to send his three daughters here to school next year.

Doctor Paul White and his family arrived at Mvumi on 5 March 1938 and after all the years of asking for a doctor, Mvumi finally had a doctor for its hospital. John reported the event saying 'Dr White seems a splendid and enthusiastic evangelist as well as medical worker'. Paul White went on to write a number of books based on his experiences in Mvumi but in 'Doctor of Tanganyika', one of the most autobiographical, he gives just one description of a meeting with Archdeacon Briggs:

> One evening, during my first month in Mvumi, I sat drinking coffee that had been grown near the shores of Lake Victoria Nyanza. The wind blew noisily through the baobab trees, a loose piece of corrugated iron rattled intermittently, and in the native village donkeys brayed and drums throbbed. It was all very strange to me, but to the veteran CMS pioneer, Archdeacon Briggs, who had spent forty-seven years in Ugogo, they were everyday sounds.
>
> He was sharing our evening meal. ... He told me of the days when he first came out and walked up from the coast, camping in the jungle among hostile people, and in waterless desert. I heard of serious illness with no doctor available, of teeth extracted by

the patient himself, of adventures with animals, insects, floods and famines. I looked with a new understanding at this intrepid pioneer, and felt that our new home really had all modern Tanganyikan conveniences.

I fell into a reverie, and thought of the Archdeacon's doings from a variety of angles. Chicken – tough and tasteless, costing threepence and worth about half that sum – had been the main meat portion of his diet for nearly half a century. His carving of the scraggy birds was a pleasure to watch. Ponderously I worked it out in my head: 2 by 50 by 365. 'About thirty-six thousand dead chickens' I murmered aloud.

'Pardon?' said the pioneer.

I looked up guiltily. 'Sorry, Sir. I was just working out how many chickens you must have carved since you arrived in Tanganyika!'

Health issues were pressing in on both John and Annie. Only a short time after Paul White's arrival, on 8 May 1938, John wrote to London saying:

For some time I have been trying to face up to the question of whether I ought to continue my duties of Secretary of the Mission owing to my advancing years and my strength not being what it used to be. A rather stern reminder came to me a few months ago when I became seriously ill with what the Doctor (Dr White) has diagnosed as a slight attack of angina pectoris, brought on by high blood pressure. I have been on a rather drastic diet for a couple of months and my blood pressure has improved but I still have to be careful, and I find I cannot do what I used to be able to do.

John then informed the Committee in London that he had resigned as Secretary, but asked to remain on, and recorded his gratitude 'for all your kindness to me'.

The following day John sat down and wrote to the Council in Australia, letting them in turn know that he wished to offer his resignation as Secretary:

I am now in my 71st year and my strength has been considerably reduced by a serious illness from which, even now, I have not

completely recovered. Added to that Miss Duncan my very effi-
cient assistant is due to go on leave ... the help which is available
is not sufficient to enable me to carry on, and so I feel that under
the circumstances I must make way for a younger man.

In the future, in addition to the care of Mvumi Station and
district, I am hoping at the Bishop's invitation to devote my
remaining years, if God graciously allows me to continue here for
some time yet, to completing the Bible and Prayer Book in the
Cigogo language, and I would ask your prayers for this important
work.

The only record I have found of the events that immediately
followed these letters are in Avis Richardson's memoirs, where
she calls a chapter about 1938 'A Difficult Year'. Miss Richardson herself had been on leave in Australia and returned in April:

Several members of our staff there had serious and prolonged
illnesses that required constant and devoted nursing, in some
cases day and night for weeks. We were deeply thankful that Dr
Paul White had been with us during all those anxious months.
On the last Sunday in October, Miss Taylor commented that it
was the first Sunday since April that we did not have a European
in bed ill.

A week after I returned from home leave, school opened and
we began the second term very happily, hoping to carry out
many plans. A fortnight later a number of girls became ill
suddenly and the Doctor diagnosed tonsilitis. These girls had to
be isolated and properly nursed. The number increased so that
several dormitories had to be turned into wards for the sick. It
meant a great deal of nursing and school routine was completely
disorganised. After about two weeks of this, Miss Gelding went
down with an exceptionally severe attack of tonsilitis, combined
with malaria and chickenpox. The epidemic showed no signs of
diminishing in the school. Ninety-five girls had it all told and of
these twenty five returned to the sick room a second time, and
some even a third time.

Then my turn came and I had to go to bed, where I stayed for
the best part of three weeks. I had tonsilitis and malaria. Miss
Taylor then decided it was time to close the school. We found that
the girls who were recovering so lacked vitality that it was impossible for them to continue their school work. We intended to close

school for a month and then have a long third term, but just a day or two after closing, Miss Gelding, who apparently was recovering, collapsed and was very seriously ill for weeks. This meant that the school could not open for three months.

During all this time Mrs Briggs was very ill with rheumatic fever and tonsillitis and could have no visitors for many weeks. ... Archdeacon and Mrs Briggs with Miss Gelding left for Australia in September.

It had only been a few months before, in May, that John had written about spending his remaining years in Mvumi translating the rest of the Bible into Cigogo. In September he and Annie packed up and left so quickly that there isn't even much record of the plans. It seems that it was more an evacuation than a departure, as Annie must have been physically in very poor shape. It is ironic, and a testimony to John's staying power, that after all his years in German East Africa/ Tanganyika, he had to leave because of the health of his 51 year old wife, who was twenty years his junior.

John and Annie, sitting on the steps at Kiboriani, on what was possibly the last time they holidayed there.

Bishop Chambers did record the event in his Diocesan Newsletter of October 1938:

This month Archdeacon Briggs OBE retires after 45 years service in East Africa. He has lived among the Wagogo all the time and has become their great White Father.

I hardly like to think of the Diocese without him. Since it was formed 11 years ago, he has placed his rich experience at my disposal, and has been most generous in his appreciation of all the new developments that have taken place in recent years.

With Mrs Briggs, their home at Mvumi has always been a centre of hospitality, where every wayfarer was welcome, and where the fragrance of a most invigorating atmosphere always prevailed. They will both be greatly missed, but their work will continue in the lives of those whom they have taught and influenced.

As from September 20th when they leave Dar es Salaam the Archdeacon will be Archdeacon Emeritus instead of Archdeacon of Dodoma. May he and Mrs Briggs long enjoy their well earned rest.

Minutes of the Executive Meeting of the CMS Africa Committee, London, 15 February 1939. Item number 10.

On letter from the Venerable Archdeacon Briggs, dated Mvumi July 26 1938 reporting that in view of Mrs Briggs' ill health he was resigning his connexion with the Tanganyika Mission to settle in Australia, and on report by the Secretary, the Africa Committee recommended the following resolution, which was adopted:-

That on placing the name of the Venerable Archdeacon J H Briggs OBE on the list of the Society's retired missionaries as from January 1st 1939 the Committee record their deep appreciation of his long and devoted service with the Society.

Sailing first to East Africa in 1892 the Archdeacon has seen the work in what is now Tanganyika Territory develop from pioneer stages to a well organized and rapidly growing Church. Its growth owes much to his practical experience and unselfish devotion, and its organization still more to his administrative ability and wise counsel. For many years he acted as Secretary of the Mission, and continued in this office at the invitation of Bishop Chambers when the Australian CMS assumed responsibility for the oversight of the work in Tanganyika and the Mission administration was reorganized on a diocesan basis.

His valuable linguistic services included the translation of the Bible into Cigogo, and the Committee share the Archdeacons grief that the invaliding of Mrs Briggs has held up plans for his completion of this work.

The Archdeacon's unique services to the country and people were officially recognized by the Government in 1935, when he was granted the OBE and his long service to the church in Tanganyika has been marked by his appointment by Bishop Chambers as Archdeacon Emeritus.

The Committee pray that Mrs Briggs (who shared in her

husband's labours from 1921) may soon be restored to full health, and that God's blessing may rest abundantly upon them both in their well earned retirement.

CHAPTER 7

Marks on the Landscape

John Briggs' life work in Mvumi has left many marks on the landscape and in people's lives, even seventy years after his departure. The remnants of his wonderful and legendary garden are still there, a pleasant walk from the hill. The area is called Shamba la Bwana, the Master's field, or the Lord's field. Two gardeners, Lucas Munyangh'ali and Zebedayo Mada tended the two acres from dawn to dusk, not only watering, tilling, sowing, and reaping but also guarding it from hungry children and from wandering livestock, the hedge being little protection against cattle. Each day produce was taken up to John for the mission whilst Luka and Zebedayo were allowed a share of their work too. The crops were not only the fruit trees mentioned by Angelina Reed, but also onions, tomatoes, beans, cabbages, carrots, lettuces, and doubtless much else. After John left, the garden continued for a while providing food for the Girls School, but without his input it faded and now only the mango trees, some date palms, and vestiges of the wells remain.

The many buildings he personally designed and built, or supervised the building of – the long station house, the old church, the Pan Anglican Building, the old hospital wards – still stand, and are still in use. They are noticeably well built and particularly pleasant to be in, with such careful placing of cornerstones and foundations that even though they are all built on a hill, and even though the sudden rainstorms can erode the sandy soil fiercely, the buildings have not crumbled but stand beautifully, even after all these years.

John's name is part of local vocabulary, being a shorthand

description of the descendants of the group of native people whose lives became entwined with the mission, 'watu wa Briggs'. He was ever the provider, and the way in which he helped people is part of his legend. When the flat roofed tembe huts fell down in the rain people went to him for help, he fed and kept them until things had dried out. He provided nutritious food for the children in the pre-school kindergarten and over the years demonstrated how to grow nutritious food throughout the year. His own fine physique, tall and strong even in later years, was a good advert for the good nutrition he cared so much about, and the fine way he walked was admired and remembered all those years after he left.

His name is associated with places he habitually went to, such as Uhongo, a flat topped mountain near Chikanga peak, about 15 km north of Mvumi. He used to go there for peace and quietness, for a short retreat. He would take porters and a donkey, camping equipment, some livestock for meat and milk, no doubt some vegetables and fruit from his garden and go to Uhongo for a week or so of contemplation.

Similarly at Christmas people often talk about the games that John would organise and how he made it a true festivity. He organised sports events, running and jumping competitions, and archery, using a baobab tree as a target. (The rule was that the arrow had to stick in the trunk). Sugar cane and sweets were given as prizes. Those who had been in the service ate together but anyone could go and join the games. John had boxes of presents from which Chief Mazengo would hand out gifts for different servants of the church; a hoe, an item of clothing for children, some soap.

John's friendship with Mazengo began from the time John first visited Mvumi and negotiated with Mazengo's uncle. Soon after, in 1905, Mazengo himself became chief at a relatively young age and their relationship was very significant, in particular because they were of an age, 'rika moja'. In those early days John had a discussion group involving Chief Mazengo together with future leaders such as Nataneli Chidosa, Mika Muloli and Petero Chisota where they talked about how to look after people and how to lead them. John's belief and teaching was that leading and looking after people meant to show them love and to be concerned for their well-being, rather than beating them into submission and using fear. He taught them to be merciful and show kindness, not as a sign of weakness but as a demonstration of God's love.

John evidently practised mercy himself in his dealings with people, and in his own leadership. Andreya Lungwa had a son Petro, who was a new-born baby when the family moved from Mpwapwa with John in 1900. When John returned to Mvumi after the First World War Andereya had just died and Petro would have been about 20 years old. Petro was a member of John's household as long as John was in Mvumi, first as a laundry boy and donkey keeper, then as a cook, then later John taught him to drive the Ford Chevrolet. Sometimes Petro would drive John, at others he would be sent with the car on errands. On one occasion they were driving to Dodoma and they met a lion. (The Chevrolet was a very open car!) John told Petro not to be afraid and prayed ... the lion went. Petro was clearly a favourite of John's, which is remarkable since Petro had a big weakness for drink and let John down many times. John knew all about his failings but bore with him throughout, and although he tried to get Petro to leave the beer he never chased him out of his household nor forced him to give it up. When John left he gave Petro many personal items, but sadly these were sold off one by one in order to maintain the drinking habit.

Another member of John's household was a parrot. Rose had had three parrots and a monkey in Mamboya and since parrots can live a long time it may well have been a survivor from her Mamboya days. John kept this parrot and of course it was a very good mimic. John had a distinctive booming voice that carried very well, and the parrot could mimic his commands convincingly. The parrot would say 'washa gari, Petro' (start the car, Petro) and Petro would do as he was told. When John asked why he had started the car, he told Petro 'oh, the parrot deceived you'.

John worked with people but would also challenge them. When John heard that a Christian had made beer, someone who had been taught of the dangers of beer, then he would pay a visit, perhaps together with Mika Muloli or another senior leader. He wouldn't come in anger but he would sit down and discuss the issue, asking for the beer to be brought out. People often felt that to be caught hiding the beer would be worse so they agreed and produced it. If they agreed, then the beer would be poured out on the ground, there and then.

In 1912 John had heard that the Catholics were building at Mloa, an act of aggression on the part of the Catholics who had already agreed boundaries further south. John immediately sent 100 people to move one of his teachers there with instructions to the chief, whom he knew. These 100 people stayed one week and in that time they built a house for the teacher and a church.

John was hard working and industrious. He was given the nickname 'mwachingh'ungh'u' by the workmen who were breaking stones to build the girls school. This is the name for the bright morning star that shines in the east early in the morning as people are waking up. No doubt he was making a daily check on production to see that he wasn't paying the labourers for nothing. There was no slacking when John was around. Asani Malugu, who was born about 1917, was sent as a teenager to stay with an aunt in Mvumi so that he could attend the school, after John invited him to come and study and offered to look after him. John sometimes would give Asani sugar cane or biscuits, but also gave him books and taught him personally on religious matters. Asani had the job of sweeping

Asani Malugu in 1999

the church, and if John saw him he would call out sternly but also with humour 'Asani, kanisa ni nzuri? Kama siyo nzuri nitashika masikio!' (Asani, is the church good? If not, I will take you by your ears). This was not a physical threat, Asani related.

Asani was a promising student and had opportunities to study further but his father wanted him to marry, so he returned home. When John heard about this he came to visit Asani's father. He sat down and greeted them, and then said he had come to take Asani and that if his father refused then John would put them both in prison! Asani told me this story, but it was clear that the strong language was not fierce or scary, just lovingly firm. Not surprisingly John succeeded in persuading his father, who was an evangelist himself, and took Asani to Mvumi to work as a teacher at the primary school. Such was John's interest in each individual to the last, that before he left he called Asani and told him, in front of Mika Muloli, that he shouldn't leave the work. Asani was eventually made a priest and in the course of his work travelled to Kenya and Uganda. Without John's firm encouragement he may never have continued to develop his training.

John is remembered as being someone who listened to people and understood their problems, their customs and their way of life. He was interested in local culture, instruments and music and liked songs but couldn't sing himself. When people had been baptised John taught them to wear their sheet of material crossed under one arm and then tied over the opposite shoulder, thus binding it round their body quite securely. Pagans simply wore the sheet as a loose cloak tied over one shoulder. This change was required not only as an outward sign of a believer's intentions but also to preserve their modesty. John didn't like Christians wearing brightly coloured cloths, which were an expensive luxury and he felt was showy, however he had no objection to the girls at the Boarding School wearing the anklets and earrings that were part of their traditional adornment. Black cloth was the cheapest and when someone became a teacher he gave them a kanzu (a simple robe) of black cloth. A senior teacher such as Mika Muloli was given a white kanzu.

John is remembered as someone who had forward ideas and

was ahead of his time. He paid people to farm sweet potatoes (a drought resistant crop which they would not otherwise have grown) in order to provide for the girls at the Boarding School. These potatoes were then dried and used all through the dry season.

John was a very generous man and a great provider for others, described to me as an 'mtajiri', a rich man. He was especially generous with food. He may have been very careful in his use of money and resources but he didn't scrimp, and this particularly applied to food. John's cook often had food to give away from the table for those in need.

There are various stories told about John concerning his departure. I was told that he had two very fine guns and that he was an excellent shot. Legend is that he would shoot some game for the pot from Mvumi hill, and then just tell people where to go and get it. These two guns he is said to have given to his old friend Mazengo as a parting gift. He gave some of his cattle to Mika Muloli; cows are wealth in Ugogo, so what better way to thank Mika for his faithful, honourable and diligent service than by giving him cattle?

There was a farewell service in the Church which was led by John and at which Bishop Chambers was present. John told the people that they should not let go of God and referred to the passage in Isaiah where God is likened to a mother hen guarding her chicks. He must have felt that they were very vulnerable. John warned them that he was leaving and in the days to come life would be hard; those who didn't study would have problems because the world was changing. He exhorted them to hold on fast to God's word. People were used to him leaving to go on journeys but he had always returned. They could not understand that he would not be coming back, because he had become a native of Mvumi. He kept cows and had fields, it was not possible for people to understand why he might leave or to accept that he would not be returning. To get the message across he tried to explain, he said he was going and not returning, but he began to cry, and this started many people crying. The story told is that he left the church with a cloth (probably a handkerchief) over his face, he was taken to a car and driven away.

'Aliagana na watu upendo mkubwa, huzini kwa yeye na kwa watu.' Asani Malugu

(He parted from people with great love, there was sadness on his part and on everyone's part).

CHAPTER 8

And Afterwards

John and Annie left the shores of Tanganyika for the last time, and headed for Annie's home in Sydney, Australia. It is hard to imagine how John could have contemplated starting life all over again, a life away from Mvumi. It is ever harder to adapt as we age, and John went from being a well known, influential, central figure in the region around Mvumi to being largely unknown and retired. He went from the pattern of rainfall, crops and harvests, drums and insects of the plains of Ugogo, to the suburban life of Sydney. Bereaved of completing his life's work, the full translation of the Old Testament into Cigogo, and having to set up home in a continent in which he had never lived before, I imagined that he faded away and that the loss overwhelmed him. But John was someone who never did things by halves.

John and Annie rented a house in Normanhurst, (1 Harris Road) a suburb of Sydney. Annie was the eighth of nine children and she had at least two sisters living quite close by. Not only that, but the next suburb, Wahroonga, was the area she had been living when she applied to CMS twenty years before, so no doubt she was familiar with the neighbourhood and perhaps particularly some of the long serving church members.

So what did they do with themselves after so many years of activity, focus and direction? They took up another part of the same life work, that of building up the church. They lived half a mile from a young Anglican church called St Stephen's, begun in 1920 by a small group of people who had put up a simple brick building for the growing community. It was still part of the parish of Wahroonga and was by no means well resourced, getting perhaps weekly pastoral visits from the curate and one service a week. A familiar situation for John and Annie after all.

The Second World War started shortly after John and Annie settled down and this meant that the church was even more hard pressed. Many clergy went off to the war as chaplains, and the rector of Wahroonga became ill. As an ordained man, John soon had plenty to do. Archdeacon Briggs, as he continued to be known, began attending the Church Committee meetings and was elected as churchwarden in 1940, since there were no other suitable younger men available for that role. He was active in assisting the clergy, especially in scripture teaching.

A young girl in her early teens called Rosalind, who lived in the parish at the time, was one of those who was profoundly affected by John and Annie's care and interest in her. They often entertained her after school and were very concerned for her when she fell from a tree and was injured, taking time with her and helping her. Through the time they spent with her they led her to a personal faith in Christ, and John was her godfather when she was subsequently baptised. John and Annie were like grandparents to Rosalind and she regarded them so, with warm affection. Rosalind remembered Archdeacon Briggs as a kindly old gentleman, tall and well-built with good carriage, crowned with snowy white hair, a real Father Christmas, happy and spry. She remembered his wide impish smile, which sprang from a boyish humour and a genuine love of children. Though to her he didn't seem to age, he did sometimes walk slowly (of course he didn't have a car again). She remembered that John and Annie were devoted to each other and she remembered that their house was called 'Mvumi'. So, in fact, the picture of John and Annie in retirement is of a warm, happy and fulfilled life lived at a more suitable pace for their progressing age and health.

Way back in this story, I told you about John's only surviving child, Joan, who was left somewhere in England after her mother Rose died so tragically in 1904. Joan was coming up to three years old then, and from John's return to East Africa in 1905 she is not referred to in any official documents again. What on earth happened to her? I am reasonably sure that she was left in the care of Rose's oldest brother, Thomas Colsey. At the time that Rose died he was about 41 years old, and a journalist. He had been married for 15 years or so but had only one child, a ten year old daughter called Dorothy Rose. They were living in Upper Tooting, South West London, and had a household that included a servant so they were in a position to provide a home for Joan. Their daughter, Dorothy, was born about the time that Rose left to go to East Africa so no doubt Dorothy Rose was named in her honour.

When John visited England on his next leave in 1910 he wrote a letter 'c/o T Colsey', who by that time had moved to Sutton. So we will hope that Joan's childhood was happy and well-provided for, and that she did get occasional glimpses of her father.

The next trace of her is when she married Walter George Ward, a 'Mining Engineering Company's Buyer'. They married in Birmingham in September 1927, he aged 26, she aged 25 and, surprisingly, they married in a Catholic Church. Who knows what John thought of this, or if he even met Walter? His previous leave had been a couple of years before, and by the time he visited again in 1930 the marriage was over. Walter divorced Joan on the grounds of adultery with a J W Y Colsey, but since the only grounds for divorce at the time was adultery that is not necessarily what happened. Since Colsey is an unusual name, the Mr Colsey in question was undoubtedly a relative, and may have agreed to have his name used in order to help her out of a difficult situation. All we can conclude is that the marriage was not happy.

The mystery is this. Why did John and Annie not retire to England where he had a daughter? It seems as if she had become somehow disinherited. It seems strange that a man who, throughout his life demonstrated a love for children and a great personal interest in them, a man who had a great capacity to forgive, seems to have neglected his own daughter. Of course, it may not be so. It may be that she was happy and well provided for, that she didn't need them. It may have been that Joan herself thought they would be better off in Australia where the climate is a little more tropical. But there is one last question.

John and Annie lived quietly but productively at their new 'Mvumi' for a number of years, but then John's health did decline. The angina that he had mentioned in 1938 persisted and then he started to suffer from gallstones and infection of the gall bladder. He died in St Luke's Hospital, Darlinghurst, on 11 February 1944 after a major operation, just a few days after his 76th birthday. For such a remarkable life, little remark was made of his death. When John left Mvumi in 1938 CMS in England had not published any account of his 46 years on the field, despite this number of years service seeming to be something of a record, at least for the region. Neither did CMS in England publish an obituary on John's death, nor even a two line note of the occasion. The only obituary was written in the Australian CMS publication, Open Door:

> Archdeacon Briggs was sent to Ugogo to establish a mission station at Mvumi. There he began a work which will always be his memorial. In an inhospitable part of Tanganyika he founded a work which today comprises one of the largest mission stations in the centre of the diocese of Central Tanganyika, and which has become famous for its hospitality to both European and African alike. Mvumi was Archdeacon Briggs' creation and is now his monument, for he went to it as a dry and thirsty land and left it a place of plenty.

John was buried in Macquarie Park Cemetery, in a simple grave amongst thousands of others. His headstone reads

In Loving Memory of
John Henry Briggs OBE
Archdeacon
Died 11th Feb 1944 aged 76 years
CMS Missionary in Tanganyika 46 years

John wrote his last will just four months before he died, in which he left 'everything' to Annie. 'Everything' comprised a 3 foot bedstead and bedding, a chest of drawers, some books, and £95 19/6 in a current account at the local bank. It is humbling to consider how little in the way of worldly possessions he had at the end of such an illustrious life. He owned no property, no cows, no vegetable garden, just some books, a bed, a chest of drawers and some savings carefully put on one side to be able to live with dignity. There is no mention of Joan in John's will, even though she is mentioned on his death certificate as issue of his first marriage: 'Joan R, 42 years, living'. Perhaps it was for pragmatic reasons that she was left out of the will; it was the war, she was far away. But the question is left hanging there, what about Joan?

It was not possible for me to meet John Briggs as I would love to have done and to have heard him tell the story, so I started digging; digging out the words written at the time, digging out the records, digging out the living memories of the oldest people, those who could remember him. I have strained with eyes and ears to pick up distant messages and at the end of it all I have enormous respect for John Henry Briggs. He came from humble beginnings, he showed sufficient ability and dedication to be trusted to an immensely difficult task at a young age, he proved equal to that task and despite severe hardships his mental stability never seemed to waver. He used his practical skills to benefit all wherever he went, be it in building well, growing well, or organising well. His self-discipline was complete, his health generally robust, his energy levels enormous. Yet he knew what it was to live with deep grief and loss, he understood human needs so well and was compassionate in his care, he expected such high standards of himself but was forgiving of failure in others.

John's life spanned remarkable changes in East Africa, from a land of tribal chiefdoms to the British Colonial Administration of the 1930's, from travelling across the country on foot to having the use of a car and a daily train service from the coast. I can't help wishing he had written it all down himself, realising what a remarkable life he had had, what remarkable stories he could tell. But of course that would not be John, and had he written at all, I know that he would not have mentioned himself. I like him for that too.

John's life was a life led quite simply in service to his Master and given to the people of Ugogo. I see evidence of only one motive, and that is love.

One memorable afternoon in Mvumi I had the great opportunity to meet and interview someone who I had heard respectfully spoken of many times, Dani Mbogoni. Dani had been a young man in John's last years, he was now quite elderly but nevertheless still an intelligent, active and able man, who had lived a long life of integrity and responsible service amongst his own people. His very presence imbued the whole occasion with dignity and reverence. I asked him about his own life first, and then I asked him about John Briggs. He launched into a speech which I recorded as fast as I could write, quite transfixed by the power with which he spoke. This is my translation of what he said:

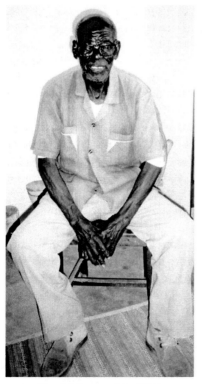

Dani Mbogoni in 1999

Briggs had a very good orderliness, it was visible in his business.

For us who were studying, he made us strong in spiritual things, in religious things.

He held us, *[Dani held out his hands expressively, palms upwards]* and he raised us up, *[he raised his hands as he spoke.]*

Even when I was at primary school he was with us,

but I was still being raised up,

but after finishing school, when I came here, I understood he really loved us.

I understood he wanted us to do whatever we did as a servant of God.

He would call us, teach us and explain.

We were quite used to going to his house.

His leadership was a good foundation

John Briggs near the end of his years in Tanganyika

Bibliography

Briggs, J. H., *In the East Africa War Zone* (CMS 1918)

Bullard, Narelle, *letters of Narelle Bullard* (held at Sydney State Library)

Chambers, G., Sibtain, N. P., *Dare to Look Up* (Sydney 1968)

Chambers, G. A *Tanganyika's New Day* (CMS 1931)

Knox, Elisabeth, *Signal on the Mountain: The Gospel in Africa's Uplands before the First World War* (Acorn Press Ltd, 1991)

Richardson, Avis, *Hold High the Torch* (published privately and held in the CMS Australia archives)

Reed, Angelina, *The Shining Cross* (CMS Archive ref CMS/ACC173 F1)

Spriggs, Ruth, *Diary* (CMS Archive ref CMS/ACC172 F1)

Westgate, R. I., Carter M., Leach D., *T.B.R. Westgate A Canadian Missionary on Three Continents* (Education and Resources Group, Boston, Massachusetts, 1987)

White, Paul, *Doctor of Tanganyika* (Paternoster Press, 1952)

Sources

CMS Archive at the University of Birmingham Library – Special Collection; including character references, copies of letters sent from the London based Parent Committee, letters written to the Parent Committee from East Africa, and Annual Letters. Also CMS publications such as *The Gleaner* and Bishop Chambers' Diocesan Letter, which are held at the CMS library. Where quoted these are all identified in the text and can be found according to the type of material and date.

Interviews conducted in 1999 with elderly people in the Mvumi area, aged over 80 and some in their 90's.

Transcriptions of interviews with elderly people in the Mpwapwa/Mvumi area, conducted in 1968 by Elisabeth Knox.

Her Majesty's Court Service, Principal Registry of the Family Division

Office for National Statistics, General Register

State Records, New South Wales, Australia

New South Wales Register of Births, Marriages and Deaths

Printed in the United Kingdom
by Lightning Source UK Ltd.
133417UK00001B/16-72/P

9 780956 046703